THE ENGINEERING

OF COINCIDENCE

a scientific explanation of magic

Robert Ramsay

"One man's 'magic' is another man's engineering.
'Supernatural' is a null word."
— Robert A. Heinlein, The Notebooks of Lazarus Long

"It's still magic even if you know how it's done."
— Terry Pratchett, A Hat Full of Sky

Introduction

Tomorrow, you have a job interview. It's for your dream job; not only have you wanted this job for a long time, you know in your heart of hearts that you can do it better than anyone. Interviews can go badly, though. Interviewers can be bad tempered. They might hate your tie.

You need something extra. You need good luck. You might carry a lucky charm. You might sleep with your CV under your pillow. You find some object, some act, that represents your desired success.

The day comes, and the interview goes really well. On your way home, you get a call - you got the job! As you put your phone back in your pocket, you feel the lucky charm, you remember the CV under the pillow. You have used magical techniques to bring you the luck you needed.

Naturally, this is usually dismissed as superstitious rubbish; how could there be any rational explanation of such a thing? And yet bookshops are full of books about this 'magic'. They call themselves 'self-help', 'spiritual guidance' or even 'management skills', but ultimately, magic is what they rely on. These books are united by one thing: they all tell you how to do the magic, in a thousand different ways, but none of them really explain how this life-changing power works, and the reason for that is simple.

They don't know.

The subject of this book is magic, and the purpose of it is to explain how it works.

At the age of twenty-three, I was feeling depressed and aimless about my future. I'd recently been made redundant, and although I was lucky enough to get a new job soon after, being unemployed made me think hard about what I wanted to achieve with my life, since I didn't feel that I'd achieved a great deal thus far. A friend of mine had got some free tickets to see the film "Dead Poets Society", starring Robin Williams, about a schoolteacher who inspires his class to make something of their lives. Seeing this film was like a lightning bolt passing through me; the inspiration that Robin Williams' character brought out in the students was the same inspiration that was suddenly kindled in me. I came out of the cinema vowing to "Carpe Diem" (Latin for "seize the day") (not realising that this was originally Romantic Poet code for "Time's short; let's fuck!").

I was realistic enough about my abilities to know that I would never be world-class at any of the things I liked to do. I was not going to be the next Picasso, the next Hendrix, the next Hemingway. I realised my only choice was to dedicate myself to doing something that no-one else had done yet.

I've always been interested in finding out how things work; I learned to read quite early, and a set of children's science encyclopedias was one of my first presents. The idea that it was possible to explain the mysteries of the world using science was a thrilling and seductive notion for me. In parallel with this, I enjoyed reading ghost stories, both fictional and reported. The sense of mystery that these stories gave me was very similar to the thrill I got from reading about science. As time went on, I discovered that ghosts weren't the only phenomena that people claimed to have experienced that seemed to be outside the field of science. Telekinesis, telepathy, remote viewing, and, most of all, incredible coincidences that people seemed to have created, either accidentally, or by strange rituals. And I wasn't the only person to show serious interest in these seemingly inexplicable things.

Carl Jung, the famous psychiatrist, had a patient whose

treatment he was struggling with, because whatever the subject, she always knew better. At one point, she was describing a dream in which a friend gave her a piece of jewellery shaped like a golden scarab. At that moment, Jung heard a tapping on the window behind him. When he opened the window, a large insect flew in. Jung caught the insect, and found that it was a rose-chafer beetle, of an iridescent gold-green colour. He handed it to the woman, saying "Here is your scarab". It was an enormous shock to her, and as Jung dryly observed: "The treatment could now begin with satisfactory results."

Jung went on to collaborate with the Nobel Prize-winning physicist Wolfgang Pauli on a theory of coincidence he called 'synchronicity', proposing that what we see as coincidences are surface manifestations of a deeper level of reality. Jung claimed that telepathy, clairvoyance etc. were all examples of synchronicity. So synchronicity was considered not just to be passive like the appearance of the scarab - it could somehow be directed to make these paranormal events occur.

There were even fringe groups of scientists (although many of the scientists themselves, like Pauli, were quite famous and respected in other fields) that investigated these kind of events, and had been doing so since the end of the 19th century. They called it parapsychology, believing that these seemingly inexplicable occurrences were caused by hitherto untapped powers of the human mind, and they set up various parapsychological societies to study these powers. By the time I joined one of these societies (the SPR - the Society for Psychical Research), scientists and investigators of various stripes had been producing papers on the subject of parapsychology for almost a hundred years. I vividly remember the first time I looked through the SPR Library; there were shelves and shelves of investigations, papers; so much documentation, from all over the world, that I thought to myself: "There has to be something to this; something real."

I came to the conclusion that if these events really happen, and aren't just hoaxes or figments of peoples' imaginations, then there had to be an undiscovered scientific explanation behind them. If Jung were correct, it should be possible to manipulate synchronicity; to interact with a deeper level of reality. You could take advantage of naturally occurring events to 'make things happen'. Normally, this would be described as 'magic'. I would be searching for the scientific explanation of magic; this was the thing that no-one had done yet. And if I found a convincing explanation that showed that it didn't exist? That would also be a success.

So, when I talk about magic; what am I really talking about?

I'm not talking about stage magic where a lot of skill and hard work goes into making seemingly impossible things appear to happen. Watches disappear and reappear, people are sawn in half, and the playing card that you chose a minute ago seems to have travelled halfway round the world. None of this involves paranormal powers - they are called magic tricks because that is exactly what is happening; we are being tricked and we know it, and that is what makes stage magic so entertaining.

At the same time, I'm not talking about the kind of magic that we see in film and on TV where people turn into dragons or fling fireballs at each other, in clear violation of all known laws of physics. This is massively unrealistic and has severely affected our expectations of actual magic. As we shall see, real wizards are, unfortunately, not as exciting and powerful as pretend wizards. To paraphrase Bill S. Preston Esq.: "We were heinously lied to by our album covers!"

The 20th century magician Aleister Crowley (described both as 'Magic's Picasso' and 'The Wickedest Man in the World') defined magic as "causing change to occur in accordance with one's Will". This turns out to be a very smart definition, since it covers two kinds of change; normal actions (potato farming and tax collecting were two of Crowley's examples) and the kind of 'making things happen' that we normally associate with 'magical magic', such as performing a secret ritual of some kind to get that new job.

Crowley underlined this by saying "Every intentional act is a Magickal Act." He also spelled it with a 'k' (as it was in occult treatises of the 1600's) to avoid confusion with stage magic. (I'm not going to bother following Crowley's spelling, as I'm hoping this introduction will suffice to dispel any confusion about what sort of magic I'm talking about.)

Normally, we decide to do something, and we act on it without considering it to be anything miraculous. We choose food in a restaurant, we choose a job to apply for, we choose our path through life through our actions. This is 'normal' magic; desired outcomes achieved through the implementation of our will.

'Magical' magic is similar, except in this case: the choosing we do translates into a result without (seemingly) an intervening chain of cause and effect. No-one has explicitly acted on your desire, no-one except you may even know about it. There is the magic you did to express your desire, and then there is the fulfilment of that desire.

This is normally called 'luck'.

The author, comic writer, and magician, Alan Moore, had one of his characters, the magician John Constantine, refer to magic as "the science of coincidence" because he had the literary conceit that the character lived in a universe where they knew how magic worked, so there was already a 'theory of magic' in that universe, permitting Constantine to describe magic as a science.

In our universe, we have no such theory. So magic is, currently, purely a practical subject like the building of cathedrals during the Middle Ages; they tried all kinds of building methods. The ones that worked - the cathedral stayed up. The ones that failed - it fell down. So I put forward, in addition to Crowley's definition; that the 'magical' part of magic should be defined as not the science, but "the *engineering* of coincidence"; since when you successfully build things, it becomes engineering.

(I could have called it, in deference to Jung, "the manipulation of synchronicity", but since all that Jung really knew about synchronicity was that it involved coincidence, this would have been a circular definition.)

With regard to there being no theory of magic; this is because magicians have never known how (or indeed why) magic works. Many magicians have had complex and involved systems that purport to explain magic, but almost all of them are just belief systems; sometimes rigorously self-consistent, but, ultimately, explaining nothing.[1]

Even Aleister Crowley stated that you don't need to know how a tractor works in order to drive one - thus he was not only admitting that he didn't know how magic worked, he was also implying that he had no interest either, possibly because of the common assumption that magic is 'supernatural' i.e. outside any laws that apply to the normal universe. Once you have decided that any kind of materialism *cannot* explain magic, you have no motivation to seek explanations, since any explanation that relates to ordinary reality would not only be superfluous, but completely impossible if the magic were truly supernatural. For example, I've met people who desperately wanted the existence of magic validated, (so that they would be taken seriously), but not to have the nature of the magic explained, even though that is the very thing that would allow them to be taken seriously.

Really though, as Robert Heinlein put it: 'supernatural' is a null word. It can be translated as 'something that does not exist' - if a thing exists, it must be natural. Supernatural is a thing which is beyond nature, not natural, and thus, does not exist. If magic (and magicians) are to be taken seriously, there needs to be an explanation of magic that forges a link to the known scientific explanations that have served us so well.

I'm not talking about vague references to 'the ether' or 'cosmic energies' or any of the other models that magicians have fashioned out of whole cloth to make their magic sound more legitimate and/or scientific. Even in 'ordinary' science, you can only experiment and collect data for so long before you need a theory to provide some kind of consistent explanation for your

[1] The only magician I know of that has made a serious attempt to marry physics and magic is Peter J. Carroll, author of PsyberMagick and The Octavo.

results. And if those results are strange and inconsistent (as they often are in parapsychology - the scientific study of magical effects) then your theory needs to explain the inconsistencies in a consistent manner. Hopefully, that theory will then go on to make some verifiable predictions!

I won't be claiming that any of our current physical theories are wrong - quite the opposite in fact; only by taking our most successful theories seriously can we hope to understand what they truly mean. This is quite normal in physics; the history of physics is full of discoveries where the theory explains the observations, but ends up going against what we normally call 'common sense', because our common sense is filled with faulty assumptions. As Douglas Adams said: "Assumptions are those things we don't know we're making."

One of the biggest problems arises when people treasure their assumptions over the facts. You have to have assumptions, of course; they are part of the scaffolding around which we build our ideas. At the same time, they need to be dismantled when they are no longer of any use. For example, every time more and more detailed observations were made about the movement of the planets, before Copernicus showed that the Earth revolved around the Sun, people just added more and more rotations inside the planets' orbits ('epicycles') to explain how the planets weaved back and forth in the night sky, instead of simply abandoning the incorrect basic assumption that everything revolved around the Earth.

It should be easy to tell when your assumptions are at fault; you think you have a paradox. Normally, we wouldn't even call it a paradox - the word implies that two equally true things contradict each other - we just need to realise that one of the two things is wrong. As Richard Feynman put it: "The 'paradox' is only a conflict between reality and your feeling of what reality 'ought to be.'"

The trick lies in being able to spot which assumptions are implicit in the 'ought to be' part; the ones that require us to break down our experience of the universe and rebuild it, so that it matches up with what physics tells us. As Carl Sagan said: "To make an apple pie from scratch, one must first create the universe."

My basic assumptions are these:

1. The Universe we experience exists, and is real. This seems obvious, but it means is that the Universe exists independently of us; if we were not here, there would still be a Universe.

2. The theories of physics we have are correct (if not necessarily complete). Physicists (and journalists for that matter!) receive missives daily from people who claim to have 'proved Einstein wrong' and suchlike. To avoid being lumped in with them, any explanation of magic must not contradict our known successes.

3. Whatever the explanation for these strange events and experiences, they cannot all just be dismissed out of hand. Any explanation should not negate someone's genuine experience.

We are going to combine four areas of science, in order to get our 'new' explanation of the universe: relativity, quantum physics, entropy, and chaos theory.

Relativity is the science of space and time. Quantum physics is the science of very small things, and how they build up into large things. Entropy is the science of possibilities and disorder. Chaos theory is the science of complexity.

Once we have rebuilt our view of the universe, we can use it to shed light on why we experience the world the way we do. Then we can see how it is possible, in this view, for magic to be created.

All of this forms the 'Theoretical Magic' part of the book.

The second part is 'Practical Magic'. Not a book of spells, but an examination of some ancient and modern magical techniques to show how well they match up (or don't) with the magical model that the previous section has derived.

Thirdly, I speculate on some of the directions this theory and practice might lead us.

The purpose of this book is not to persuade you. If you are dead set against the idea that what we normally call 'chance' can be manipulated (no matter how difficult or limited that manipulation might be), then no amount of words from me will shift you.

We need to know how the tractor works. That is the purpose of this book; to *explain* how this magic, this engineering of coincidence, *could* be possible, and what current mysteries it might explain, given what we already know about how the universe works, and the way that we experience that universe.

I'm hoping you can keep an open mind to follow the explanations in the book right to the end, and that it will give you some interesting things to think about. At the very least, I hope you will not resort to St. Augustine's final argument against the existence of other Earth-like worlds: "God forbid!"

PART 1: Theoretical Magic

Relativity

Everyone's heard of Albert Einstein. The most famous and iconic physicist of the 20th Century; creator of both the Special and the General Theories of Relativity, one of the founders of quantum theory, and the man who proved that atoms were real things (lacking direct evidence, many 19th century chemists and physicists did not actually believe in atoms).

It's his 1905 Special Theory of Relativity I'd like to concentrate on.

The Special Theory explains that there is no privileged point in the Universe from which events are measured; all events are relative between two or more observers. What this means, is that if two people are moving at different speeds and/or in different directions, they will not be able to agree on when 'now' is, because each of them will have their own personal 'now'.

Relativity has two assumptions: 1) The speed of light is the same for all observers and 2) the same rules apply to everyone, no matter where they are or how fast they are moving. How time passes in the universe outside your immediate surroundings is dictated by how fast you are travelling. The faster you travel, the slower your time passes from the viewpoint of anyone travelling slower than you! For you, of course, they are the ones whose time is passing faster, whilst you feel completely normal! Similarly, if the slower people measure your spacecraft from outside, they will find that it is shorter (in the direction of travel) than it was when it was standing on the ground. You, of course, travelling in that ship, will feel fine and not squashed at all - it will be everyone else who appears to be stretched out! Your mass will also be increasing with speed until it gets to the point where it would take an infinite amount of energy to accelerate your spacecraft to the speed of light. It took someone as clever as Einstein to work this out because at normal speeds, these effects are negligible. You need to be travelling at least half the speed of light before they become observable at the normal human scale, and they don't really kick in until you are travelling around 90% of the speed of light or higher.

These kind of discoveries in physics give us a glimpse of the breaking down and rebuilding that we need to do when reformulating our viewpoint. They are only shocking or perplexing because they go against our assumptions about how things work. For example, before Einstein, we assumed that travelling near the speed of light would be no different an experience than travelling at any other speed. It's a common story in physics, that the discoveries we make end up going against our 'intuitions', our assumptions, and what is usually misleadingly referred to as 'common sense'.

The other part of Special Relativity that concerns us is the nature of space and time. From the two assumptions of the speed of light and the laws of physics both being the same for everyone, Einstein showed that space and time are inextricably connected. Since people moving at different speeds cannot agree on a single 'now', all 'nows' are equally valid, and thus, equally real.

In 1908, the mathematician Hermann Minkowski created the formal mathematics that brought space and time together, combining the three dimensions of space and the single dimension of time to form a four-dimensional 'block' of spacetime. Minkowski announced this with a flourish at a lecture in Cologne: "Henceforth, space for itself, and time for itself, shall completely reduce to a mere shadow, and only some sort of union of the two shall preserve independence."

When we talk about an object having several dimensions we start from a point. A point has zero dimensions - if you were standing on that point in the middle of nowhere, you would have no freedom to move in any direction. Now we add more and more points parallel to the original point and it becomes a line. A line has one dimension. Standing on the line, you can walk up and down along it. Now we add more and more lines parallel to our original line until we get a flat plane - a surface, which has two dimensions. You can wander about on the plane as you do on the Earth. Now, we add more and more planes, again, parallel to the original. This becomes a block, which has three dimensions. With a jet pack (or if gravity was turned off) you can navigate to anywhere within this three dimensional space.

Now comes the tricky part. You have to imagine more and more blocks being added, parallel to the original block. This is a four dimensional object, usually called a tesseract. Parallel in which direction? As three dimensional creatures, we certainly can't point to it. Since this new dimension in our pile of blocks is going to represent time (duration), it's probably easiest to think of each block as a 'snapshot' of a moment, and quietly drop one of the physical dimensions so you can think of this four dimensional spacetime as a big transparent block with all the snapshots embedded within it, flattened out. Here (as an example) is such a representation of a small piece of the block, where you can see all of the dancer's movements at once, as if you were 'outside' the block.

Imagine; when you look at the entire block of the 4D universe like this, you are able to see your whole life from the 'outside'. You see a long line of three dimensional snapshots of you, stretching from your birth, looping around and around as you visit the same places over and over again; then moving to loop in other places as you go to school, to home, to work, and back home again forming clusters of loops based around wherever you lived until the line peters out when you die and stop changing your relative position in spacetime.

From outside, you see all of these lines and loops at once; time would just be one of the dimensions that the lines and loops were drawn in. One of the implications of this is that everything in your life is predetermined. You would have no free will; since every action you take in your entire life is already laid out in the block of spacetime, you would be unable to deviate from the loops and lines that comprise your life.

Luckily for the possibility of our free will, relativity is not the whole picture. We already know this because general relativity has not yet been integrated with the 20th century's other great success in physics: quantum mechanics, which is what we shall turn to next.

Quantum Physics

Even if you don't know anything about quantum physics, you've probably heard that it's difficult to understand and very complex. There is a lot of mathematics involved, certainly, but this is not actually the part which gives it its difficult reputation.

The mathematics of quantum physics is well understood by now. (It was invented nearly a century ago, and its agreement with observation and experiment is so great, that it's been called 'the most successful theory of all time'. So much so, that almost all our modern technology from transistors to computers depends on the use of quantum mechanics). It is the meaning behind the maths that causes the problems. At the heart of it, quantum physics is supposed to be a description of what happens at the tiniest, lowest levels of matter; how the atoms that make up everything really behave - but there is a massive difference between what the maths & the observations tell us about the quantum level, and the way we see things in normal life.

There are two main conflicts with what is usually called common sense. They are the measurement problem and the problem of non-locality. These two basic problems then derive a third: how do we get from the non-intuitive quantum world to the ordinary classical world?

Firstly, the measurement problem; what it is, why it's considered a problem, and ultimately, why it shouldn't be.

The simplest experiment that shows the conflict is the 'two slit' experiment. You take two very closely placed thin vertical slits and shine a light through them to project onto a screen. What you see are a series of dark and light bands. You can think of this as being because light is made up of waves, and, just like water waves, the peaks and troughs of the two sets of waves, one set spreading out from each slit, will interfere with each other. When a peak meets a trough, they cancel out and there is darkness, but if a peak meets a peak or a trough meets a trough, they reinforce each other, and there is light.

So far, so simple. The problem begins when we try to investigate what is going on. If we measure the light to see which slit it goes through before it hits the screen, we find that it is made up of individual photons; particles of light. The dark and light bands vanish, replaced by a simple image of the two slits, and the waves seem to have magically become these single photons.

This led physicists to the conclusion that the act of measuring has to be special somehow. Before measuring, you have a 'probability wave' containing all possible paths of a single photon. The interference patterns show that we are seeing the results of all of those paths at once, even though the probability wave is considered to be just a mathematical construct.

When you measure, physicists talk about that probability wave 'collapsing' into the single course that ends up being measured. This is what causes all the confusion, and why measurement is known as 'a problem'. How can a mathematical construct 'collapse' into something real, and what is so special about the act of measuring that causes it to happen?

Some physicists claim that because the probability wave is just a construct, we cannot say anything about how real anything is in the quantum realm until after we have measured it. This interpretation of quantum measurement was first put forward by the Danish Nobel prize winner Niels Bohr, and because Bohr himself was so revered and influential (having been the first person to correctly model the atom to explain the coloured spectral lines given off by hot gases), his ideas overshadowed many other efforts to interpret the measurement problem, even into the 1960's and 1970's.

This idea that 'unmeasured things are not real' is usually called 'the Copenhagen interpretation' (because of Bohr's institute there), and is sometimes known as 'shut up and calculate', because you were not encouraged to think about what the measurements *meant*, only what they *were*. When I first started reading about quantum physics, the fact that this was considered the 'standard' interpretation of quantum physics annoyed me. Not only was this not an explanation; it was meant to actively discourage any attempt at explanation. There are clear parallels with magicians discouraging possible explanations of magic, as I mentioned in the introduction.

To illustrate the point, here's two quotes: one from Aleister Crowley, and one from Bohr's colleague Werner Heisenberg (who coined the term 'Copenhagen Interpretation'):

"In this book it is spoken of... Spirits and Conjurations; of Gods, Spheres, Planes and many other things which may or may not exist. It is immaterial whether these exist or not. By doing certain things certain results will follow; students are most earnestly warned against attributing objective reality or philosophic validity to any of them."

"we have to remember that what we observe is not nature in itself but nature exposed to our method of questioning. Our scientific work in physics consists in asking questions about nature in the language that we possess and trying to get an answer from experiment by the means that are at our disposal."

Other physicists went to the other extreme, claiming that human beings measuring things actually creates reality when the 'collapse' turns the probability wave into a single outcome. This has lead to a lot of arguments about whether a cat creates reality, or a mouse does, and so on, prompting a sarcastic response from one physicist: "Was the world wave-function waiting to jump for thousands of millions of years until a single-celled living creature appeared? Or did it have to wait a little longer for some more highly qualified measurer - with a Ph.D.?"

Let's go back to the two slit experiment. Instead of measuring which slit the light goes through to find photons (which destroys the pattern since we block the path to the screen), instead we'll turn down the light source so that it fires only a single photon at a time. We'll use a screen which will light up, and continue glowing, at the tiny point where a photon strikes it, so over time we'll see dots build up on the screen. When we do this, what we see is not images of the two slits as each photon goes through either one slot or the other. What we see is the interference pattern of light and dark bands, built up from the individual dots. Some scientists put forward the idea that this means that the photon goes through both slits at once and interferes with itself! This is not a fringe opinion, either - it is easy to find books on quantum physics that teach this 'self-interference' as the actual explanation.

There must be a better picture that explains all these strange observations without dismissing them as inexplicable or going off on strange flights of fantasy that describe the effects as being really strange, without actually explaining anything about the reasons for those effects.

So what might really be happening when the photons go through the slits?

Clearly *something* is interfering with each photon as it passes through a slit to create the interference pattern. It is a thing that acts exactly like a photon except that we cannot see it. It is as if the wave pattern, made of all possible photon paths, is still there, invisible to us - but visible to each 'real' photon as it passes through the slit and makes its way to the screen. So, there is a large group of 'shadow' photons, following all the paths that 'real' photons would, before we turned down the light source to spit out only one visible photon at a time. This phenomenon of interference happens for all kinds of particles, not just photons. So there are shadow electrons, shadow protons, etc.

What we see as 'real' is only a tiny part of what exists. The fact that we observe interference shows that these 'shadow' particles are arranged in very similar ways to our own 'real' particles. Not as some huge homogeneous lump, but as an extremely large number of 'shadow' universes, parallel to our own, each one interacting with ours only where the particles are arranged similarly enough, i.e. where the same experiment is correctly setup in each of those universes.

There is one further step. I've been talking about 'real' and 'shadow' particles as if there were some fundamental difference between them. Each of those parallel universes contains a parallel experimenter as well as a parallel experiment, and, in the same sort of way as we believe that the Earth is motionless under our feet as it hurtles through space, each experimenter automatically assumes that they are the 'real' one, and all the others are 'shadows'. Just as Einstein showed that there was no privileged place to stand with regard to observing an event, there is no privileged observer in quantum mechanics either. All of the experimenters are equally real. You can, if you like, view it as a *limitation* of the perceptions of observers. Each observer is only physically capable of observing a single universe at a time. The only way to observe the other universes is to setup experiments where they reveal themselves as 'shadows'. This explanation is usually referred to as the 'multiple worlds interpretation' of quantum physics, since every possible outcome results in a separate 'shadow' world.

This brings us to the thought experiment known as Schrödinger's Cat (I would like to point out beforehand that no-one has, to the best of my knowledge, ever been cruel enough to perform the experiment with a real cat - it can be done just as well with an equivalent experiment that uses photons or even coins).

A cat is sealed in a box. Inside the box with the cat is a poison capsule. If the capsule breaks, the cat will die. There is a mechanism attached to the capsule that will break it if it is triggered by a single radioactive atom decaying. The atom has a fifty percent chance of decaying within one minute.

The trigger mechanism is switched on, left for a minute, then switched off again.

Is the cat alive or dead after that minute?

The obvious answer is that there is a fifty percent chance of it being alive and a fifty percent chance of it being dead, and you won't know which it is until you open the box.

However, because the outcome has been made dependent on a quantum level event (the decay of a single atom), the answer actually depends on whichever explanation of quantum physics you subscribe to. The 'normal' (i.e. seemingly paradoxical) interpretation of quantum physics says that, being unobserved, the cat is in a superposition of both alive and dead until the box is open and the waveform is 'collapsed'. We now know that this is completely the wrong way of looking at it. Whilst the minute is elapsing, two different sets of microscopic timelines are building up as we go through all the possible times during that minute that the atom might decay. One set of timelines where the cat is dead, and the other set where it is still alive. You can imagine these two sets like a mixture of oil and water separating out over the course of the minute. There is a version of you in each set, and you discover which of those versions you are by opening the box.

The second collision between quantum physics and 'common sense', is the non-locality of quantum events. For this, I need to explain an important part of quantum physics called entanglement.

When two particles are separate, measuring them results in any combination of their possible states. If particles A and B each have possible states 1 and 2, then you might get (A=1 B=1), or (A=1 B=2), or (A=2 B=1), or (A=2 B=2). Measuring A on its own gives you no clue as to the value of B, and vice versa.

However if A and B then interact with each other, they become *entangled* and this limits the number of results you can get when you measure them. In our example, for the entangled A and B, you might only get (A=1 B=1) or (A=2 B=2). Now, measuring the value of A allows you to know what the value of B is without measuring it. This is an extreme example, but in general, entanglement means that measuring one entangled particle will always give you some information about the other one.

The non-locality experiment goes like this: the experimenter chooses a particle which decays into two particles, A and B, which then shoot off in opposite directions until they are a large distance apart. Because they were created from the same particle, they form an entangled pair and their combined spin directions have to add up to zero.

Spin is a property of all particles, that underlies the mechanism of magnetism (although if the particle was actually spinning, its surface would have to be moving faster than the speed of light; ordinary spinning is only an *analogy* for quantum spin), and has different values depending on what kind of particle it is; for example, electrons, protons and neutrons have half-integer spins whilst photons have whole integer spins.

If you measure the spin on A, you instantly know what B's spin will be, because 1) they are entangled and 2) the combined result has to be zero. Why is this considered a problem? Because A and B could be light years apart when A's spin is measured, it seems to imply there was faster than light communication between the two particles, since, being quantum entities, neither of them have any definite spin value before you measure them. This naive interpretation implies the instant that A's spin value was measured, making it definite, A somehow 'let B know' what that spin value was.

As explained above, entanglement places limitations on what can be observed about the particles. Thus, you too are restricted in the result set of universes you are allowed to end up in, with respect to the two particles. No faster than light communication has occurred; no matter how far apart the particles are, any world you end up in will be a world in which each particle's spin value is the opposite of the other. Because everything is already in a set of timelines, you are just ending up in one particular set, with respect to the entangled particles, just as with Schrödinger's Cat. Imagine: there are two timelines for each moment as the two entangled particles speed away from each other. When you come to measure particle A, you will end up in one of these two types of timelines for that particular moment. If you measure particle A as having spin up, then the kind of timeline you end up in will have particle B as having spin down, whereas if your measurement shows particle A as having spin down, you end up in the other kind of timeline, where particle B is spin up.

These kind of limitations imposed by entanglement leads us into the third problem: if everything is quantum, why don't we experience these quantum effects in normal life?

Under the old 'everything quantum is just weird' way of looking at things, Niels Bohr et al. just waved their hands and said that quantum behaviour and classical behaviour were two different things - 'weird' quantum behaviour only happened at very small scales.

We now know that is simply not true.

The explanation leads out of quantum entanglement, and is called 'decoherence'.

'Weird' quantum behaviour can only be observed when there is coherence between the wave functions of all the entities involved; the interference pattern from the two slit experiment is a good example - the wave functions of all the photons as they go through the slits are still coherent.

Decoherence happens when these quantum entities start interacting with the environment - becoming entangled with it. At that point, the quantum coherence of the entities spreads to that environment. As they get entangled together, we lose the coherence of the original system because it is now part of the environment. When we try to measure which slit the photon has gone through (for example), that photon is now entangled with our measuring apparatus; mixed in, like a single drop of blood falling into the ocean. The quantum behaviour that produced the interference pattern on the screen has been lost forever inside a much bigger system.

Most of the time, this means that quantum effects don't appear at macroscopic levels - even if a tiny dust grain were put into a superposition of two different locations right next to each other, interacting with its environment (i.e. colliding with air molecules) will cause it to decohere in the order of 10^{-31} seconds - a million times faster than light travelling across a proton! Again, it's easy to see why we don't see anything quantumly strange about normal life - when we watch a movie, 1/24 of a second is quite quick enough for us not to notice the difference between still images and a continuous narrative.

This is still not the whole story of how the quantum becomes classical, however. When you measure something about a quantum entity, there are always a number of choices about what to measure. Position, speed or maybe location. Anything you can measure about the entity, that information gets copied from that entity into the environment. The more copies generated of a particular kind of information, the more amenable it is to being measured, because there is less and less chance of it being scrambled in the way that quantum superpositions get scrambled.

This proliferation of copies is called 'quantum Darwinism' since the information that survives decoherence best is the information with the most copies. That information is what becomes 'classical behaviour' - enough copies have been created of non-scrambled data for the superpositions of 'weird' quantum behaviour to have been completely overwhelmed and leave only the classical data to be measured.

One last thing about decoherence. Earlier I argued that the universe we perceive is only one of a number of similar copies, whereas decoherence seems to only be talking about how classical behaviour arises in a *single* universe.

There are two more things about quantum Darwinism that it

needs to fulfil in order to agree with classical behaviour. Firstly there have to be enough copies so that everyone who measures the same information gets the same result, and secondly, each copy measured has to not interfere with the other copies.

Ultimately, this means that measuring each copy leads to each person experiencing a different outcome, 'using up' one of the copies, and so that outcome does not then affect the other outcomes from the same event.

In other words, each person associated with each copy is following a separate path; a parallel universe, just as I talked about earlier.

Quantum physics and general relativity are both amazingly successful in their separate areas, but no-one has yet succeeded in satisfactorily combining them - this would result in a theory of quantum gravity (which would be useful for investigating black holes, the nature of the Big Bang and any other extreme gravitational situation where quantum effects can no longer be ignored).

We can, however, look at the above non-paradoxical explanations of quantum behaviour to give us some clues. John Wheeler (who coined the term 'black hole', and was also the supervisor of Hugh Everett III, formulator of the original multiple worlds interpretation) and Bryce deWitt (the first populariser of Everett's interpretation) did indeed attempt to combine quantum physics and relativity to discover quantum gravity. What they ended up with, however, was the Wheeler-deWitt equation, which showed that combining the two theories objectively completely did away with any concept of change over time. Unfortunately this meant that it was useless for quantum gravity calculations and was mostly discarded or ignored. You can't investigate how things change over time using a framework that says they don't.

What their equation *does* do, however, is to give us a view of the multiverse from the *outside* (if there were such a thing as outside the multiverse); a giant, multidimensional 'block' containing every possible timeline from the beginning of the multiverse at one end, stretching out to however the Universe finishes, at the other end, with time purely as one of the measurable dimensions.

Our usual four dimensions (three of space and one of time) are inadequate to encompass this structure that contains everything. So how do we add more dimensions?

It was difficult enough to try and imagine four dimensions, but now we have to imagine those four dimensional blocks multiplied and laid out at right angles to each other, and then *that* arrangement multiplied and laid out at right angles in higher and higher dimensions of space. By the time you have enough dimensions to represent every possible arrangement of all the particles in the universe, you end up with what is known as a 'Hilbert Space', after the mathematician David Hilbert. It's often used because it allows normal geometric operations to be generalised over huge numbers of dimensions. In quantum physics, for example, each quantum state can be represented as a vector (a line with length and orientation) in Hilbert space, so that quantum interactions can be calculated by mathematical operations on the vectors that represent the actual quantum entities.

This new, higher dimensional, 'block' sheds light on the problem that relativity showed us earlier. Instead of there being a single deterministic timeline for all, stretching from birth to death, as in relativity alone, there are now a huge number of deterministic timelines for each person, the equivalent of all the possible photon paths in the beams of the two slit experiment. At countless decision points, each version of each person will only experience a single timeline, but that single timeline is built from pieces of each of the constantly dividing timelines, just like a film is made from individual still frames. Since, as in both film and experience, the frames change faster than we can perceive (see decoherence above for how fast that happens in real-life), each version of ourselves ends up experiencing one universe, moving forward in time, even though this passage of time - the idea that time flows - is actually a faulty perspective that might be categorised as an illusion; the same kind of illusory perspective that makes it seem like the Sun revolves around the Earth, rather than the other way around.

When you look at the world this way, you end up viewing all of the past and all of the future as just special cases of multiple universes; each universe a single frame of a timeline; your timeline made up of a particular stack of universes.

Incidentally, one of the usual objections to multiple worlds is the question "Where does the energy come from to create the split universes when they split?" (Because the original version of the multiple worlds interpretation assumes that the passage of time is a real thing, so the worlds split, and thus get created, in real time). Normally there is a degree of metaphysical dancing about to try and get around this question, but this multi-multi-dimensional block universe makes it all much simpler; the whole thing was already created with every possible split already within it.

I originally referred to this picture of the Universe/Multiverse rather tamely as 'my model', but I realise that it needs an actual name, so I will henceforth refer to it as 'the Timeless Multiverse' or 'the Timeless Multiverse model'.

So, if our multiverse is ultimately timeless, why do we experience time passing? What mechanism causes our view of things constantly changing to rise out of the multiverse's timelessness? The answer is to do with entropy.

Entropy

We are aware of two different types of time: the dimension of duration (objects must not only have length, breadth and depth but also duration, or they would not exist), and the experience we have of the passage of time. Almost every mention of time in physics refers purely to duration; if you plot the curve of a ball thrown in the air, the path of the ball can equally be backwards as forwards; time is considered as a kind of distance and has no intrinsic direction.

We clearly experience time as having a definite direction (we remember the past, but not the future, for example) but the only reference in physics to time having a direction is the Second Law of Thermodynamics, which states that the direction of the 'Arrow of Time' (so named because it points in only one direction - from past to future) is due to entropy increasing over time.

So what is entropy, and how does it relate to our experience of time passing?

You may have heard of entropy as a measure of disorder, but it's actually a measure of possibility. Entropy is the number of possible arrangements of microstates (arrangements of atoms) that can make up a single macrostate (something big enough for us to be interested in, a brick, for example). The more ways the atoms in a situation can be arranged to form the same overall macrostate, the higher the entropy. So a highly ordered object, like an egg, or a working computer, where the complex structure is extremely important (so as to keep the egg as an egg, or to make sure the computer carries on working) - these things have very low entropy, since there are a comparatively small number of permutations of atoms which allow the egg to remain whole, or the computer to keep functioning.

Now if we break the egg into some flour, and knead the resulting dough to get it ready for baking, the entropy of the mixture increases - because the dough is uniform, there are a much larger number of ways its individual molecules can be arranged and the dough, to our eyes at least, would look unchanged.

Entropy is thought of as measuring disorder because if you randomly arrange a collection of atoms, there will always be more ways to arrange them to form a disorderly thing than an ordered thing. There are many more arrangements of the egg's atoms that correspond to a broken egg (or even a meringue), than there are for the egg to be whole and unbroken.

Let's go back to our Timeless Multiverse. Each time there is a decision point, every possible outcome of that decision is represented in the paths of the giant multidimensional crystal of the multiverse. The number of outcomes increase in the time direction from the past to the future, because of the increasing numbers of arrangements in that direction.

At the microscopic level, each of these outcomes represents a different way in which decoherence (the entangling of separate quantum entities with the huge number of quantum entities which make up their environment) has panned out; when it comes to (say) a cup of coffee cooling to room temperature, the coffee's 'passage of time' comes down to its molecules becoming progressively more entangled with the environment until both coffee and air are the same temperature.

At the macroscopic level of human events, the differing arrangements of particles in each path result in the different versions of us that end up doing different things. Luckily, we are far more complex than a cup of coffee, and the order that we create in our bodies (read: very particular complex combinations of molecules) in order to stay alive, along with the actions we make in our daily lives, ends up creating even larger amounts of entropy in the world around us (thus not violating the Second Law of Thermodynamics - it is only after we're dead that we merely cool to room temperature like the cup of coffee).

This ever-increasing entropy manifests as an ever-increasing tree of outcomes, and functions as a kind of clock, so that although from the 'outside' there is no time passing, for us, who are entangled with this clock of ever increasing entropy/ outcomes, we experience the passage of time. Ever since this was proposed in a paper by two physicists, Don Page and William Wootters, in the 1980's, others have shown with experiments that the idea works. A team of Italian researchers entangled two photons in a static state, and then showed that they could use one of the photons as a 'clock' to gauge the time-evolution of the other, even though, from outside the global entangled state of both photons, nothing was changing.

As philosopher Craig Callender put it: "The universe may be timeless, but if you imagine breaking it into pieces, some of the pieces can serve as clocks for the others. Time emerges from timelessness. We perceive time because we are, by our very natures, one of those pieces"

Think of the flicker book - its passage of time is encoded in each of the pages, but we are outside the pages, so we see the whole thing as a timeless whole. Only when we flick through the pages one by one do we see the encoded passage of time come to life.

The Second Law of Thermodynamics is thus a consequence of the structure of the multiverse; in the direction that the number of outcomes increase, entropy increases, since this is how entropy is defined - the more arrangements there are that go to make up outcomes, the higher the entropy. This kind of entropy is known as 'thermodynamic entropy'. It would take a very special kind of experiment (or a staggering amount of time for it to happen by chance) for a series of outcomes to merge back together into a single outcome. Incidentally, the reason that we experience this ever-increasing entropy is that the multiverse began in a very low entropy state, so that there was (and is) plenty of opportunity for entropy to continue increasing in what we get to see as the direction of time. No-one can yet explain why everything started at such a low entropy, but they all agree that without that low entropy initial condition of the universe, there would be no galaxies, no stars, and certainly no 'us' to discuss it. We can speculate that tracing the outcomes of the Timeless Multiverse backwards, we would eventually get to a point where the entire Multiverse was composed of a single outcome. This would be the lowest possible entropy state, and thus, the beginning of our Universe. What this tells us is that this special state actually depends on the structure of the complete Multiverse, but doesn't help to explain why.

There is a second kind of entropy (although there are still arguments about whether the two types are the same). This is *informational* entropy. Discovered in 1948 by Claude Shannon (the man who invented information theory, digital circuit design, artificial learning, and a flame-throwing trumpet) he wanted to find the most efficient way of encoding a message to send to someone. Information in Shannon's context is related not to what you *do* say, but what you *could* say; information is a measure of your freedom of choice when deciding what to transmit. Shannon called information 'negentropy' - the opposite of entropy. This leads to informational entropy being defined as our degree of ignorance about a system - all the things about that system that we do not have information about.

This kind of entropy also relates to the Timeless Multiverse model. The futures of our individual timelines can be defined as the sections of the multiverse that have not yet decohered for us; the alternatives are still in superposition from our viewpoint inside the multiverse. The things we know, the things we remember, though; they belong to parts of timelines that have already decohered, and that means that the information we already have, can limit which sets of future timelines we have access to, since those futures need to contain our past so that our experiences are consistent. Any future paths which do not contain the memories from our individual timeline cannot really be said to be our future at all.

So thermodynamic entropy can be considered to be *objective* - the microstates evolve deterministically, whilst informational entropy is *subjective* - we are measuring our knowledge (or lack thereof) about chosen macrostates that contain a selection of microstates. This corresponds with the two different versions of time; the objective duration and the subjective passage of time, since the duration is ultimately measured by the difference between two amounts of thermodynamic entropy, and time passing is related to the path we take through that maze of outcomes.

I know that this picture makes normal human experience seem even more mind-boggling than it is normally - but to see just how much more, we need the next piece of the puzzle: chaos theory.

Chaos Theory

Archimedes once said "Give me a place to stand and with a lever I will move the whole world." The idea was that if the lever was long enough, and you had somewhere fixed for the lever to pivot, the strength of a man could theoretically lift the weight of the Earth. (To do so, the lever would also have to be made of a completely rigid, currently unknown (even impossible) material, and in the region of 10 million light years long - four times the distance to the nearest galaxy!)

Chaos theory shows that the right circumstances can create the equivalent of such a lever; its 'lever' is described as 'sensitivity on initial conditions'. This means that a tiny change in initial conditions can multiply up to a vast range of different consequences, the smallest change at one end of the 'lever' capable of producing wildly different results at the other end.

People normally talk about the butterfly that flaps its wings and causes a storm on the other side of the world; or a single stone, thrown from the top of a snow-covered mountain, that gathers into an avalanche that destroys an entire village in the valley below.

Regardless of butterflies, the weather itself is a good example of this sensitivity. The models we use to predict the weather become useless for more than a few days prediction, and even if we had models that were completely accurate, with a complete set of the initial data, it would still be impossible to predict the weather more than two weeks in advance, because even the tiniest rounding error in the calculations would cause enormous divergences between the model and reality the further and further into the future we try to predict.

This means that a system can be completely deterministic, mathematically speaking, and yet be impossible to predict. This is a chaotic system.

As we saw in the last chapter, every possible microscopic future is already deterministically enumerated in the Timeless Multiverse. Many of them would be, to the human eye, indistinguishable, as they differ only in the position of, say, individual atoms. Nearly all the normal events that we are interested in, however, will be macroscopic enough to occur in huge 'bundles' of timelines.

The 'sizes' of these bundles are what determines the probability of the various outcomes of the macroscopic event we are looking at - in general, the more probable the event is, the more microscopic futures will contain that event. At the microscopic level, everything is deterministic. By the time we get to our level, so much information about this microscopic level has been ignored that things become uncertain. All that remains are the probabilities of each macroscopic outcome.

When you roll an ordinary six-sided die, there will be a roughly equal number of microscopic timelines that correspond to each face coming up. At this microscopic level, the same face would be uppermost, but the die might come to rest in a slightly different position. If the die had two faces with one dot on them, there would be twice the number of timelines that correspond to a 'one' as for each of the other four possibilities. (This is true because each face, no matter what its marking, is considered to come up in an equal number of timelines to any other face).

If, however, the die were loaded to come up, say, six twice as often as any other number, there would be the same number of positional outcomes (there would not be any greater number of ways that a 'six' outcome dice can be physically arranged), but the amplitude (think of it as the 'width' of a path) of all the 'six' paths would be greater than the total of each of the 'one' to 'five' sets of paths; thus the probability does not always depend solely on the *number* of possible physical outcomes - the 'sizes' of the bundles can be increased by some of the outcomes contributing more than others, like the six on the loaded die.

Going back to the ordinary, non-loaded die, rolling it more than a certain number of times and let it bounce more than a certain number of times, one or another face coming up will be decided by a difference of less than the width of an atom between the two initial positions. So with enough rolling and bouncing, the result of the die can be considered to be indeterminate in a quantum fashion. It is events like these, that can scale up from the quantum level to the macroscopic level, that we are interested in. This is the most important aspect of the Schrödinger's Cat thought experiment - the setup allows a quantum level event (the radioactive decay of a single atom) to scale up to a macroscopic result (the death of a cat).

Luckily, not all quantum level events are capable of scaling up like this - normally they tend to cancel each other out, otherwise butterflies would constantly be causing storms all over the planet! Human beings are, however, very good at producing 'scaling events' - actions that proceed from (for example) the firing of a single neuron, that triggers a single idea, can scale up to change whole civilisations. Communism would be an extreme example: it started as an idea, then a book, and eventually shaped the history of large parts of the world.

This ability to create scaling events allows human beings to be considered as a non-linear system - the kind of system that chaos theory deals with - because the determinism of the individual universes, coupled with this sensitivity on initial conditions, makes the selection of paths through those individual universes much less deterministic in their outcomes.

We're now in a position to put all the pieces together to show how we experience the Timeless Multiverse.

The Timeless Multiverse

When Einstein dreamed up the Theory of Relativity, he began by wondering what it would be like to ride on a beam of light. When I started thinking about the Multiverse, I wondered to myself what a person journeying through this Multiverse would look like if they could see themselves 'from the outside'.

We all know what the 'inside' experience of the Multiverse looks like; we experience it every day - a single thread of experience in a constantly changing world.

Now, let's look at how this normal human experience pans out under what we've learned about the Timeless Multiverse.

Earlier, we talked about how your individual timeline is made up of pieces of countless other timelines, so that even though the complete list of those timelines is deterministic, the path that you end up experiencing through that list is not predictable.

Imagine that at each moment, you could take a snapshot of your brain activity. A picture of all the neurons in your brain, along with the electrochemical status of each one. Imagine the huge amount of data that even a single snapshot like this would need. Now imagine each moment's snapshot following one after another as you switch from timeline to timeline, carving out your path through the Timeless Multiverse.

This path, this personal timeline (recorded in our memories), passes from snapshot to snapshot like the individual pages in a flicker-book, from the front of the book to the back, from the past to the future. Except in our 'flicker-book', every time there is a human-sized choice, we can choose which of the different sets of paths to go down, that radiate from that choice. Perhaps a better image is riding in a mine cart along a massively branching railway line where we have some control of the points to allow us to influence our destination.

Thus, we do not change the universe - *we move to the place where it is changed.* (More accurately, we *experience* the place where it is changed, since the whole model is timeless.) So when I talk about 'causing' things to happen (normally or magically), I actually mean the things we do to select the path where you experience a version of yourself where they *do* happen.

This is the crux of the Timeless Multiverse. The misperception of our normal experiences can be seen as a 'figure and ground problem', like this famous vase/faces picture.

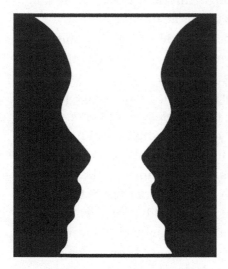

We are so used to seeing the world one way, that it can be quite a shock to see it the other way; as if you thought your world was the vase, but then discovered that actually - it's the faces. Once you can come to terms with seeing the world in this new way, understanding the process of magic will become much easier.

To introduce yet another metaphor, you can think of the multiverse as being like the world's biggest "Choose Your Own

Adventure" book, our choices moving us from page to page, forming our memories. The whole book (the Timeless Multiverse) already exists; but, due to the physical limitations of our brains, we are only able to experience the single path we take through it. Perhaps that's just as well, otherwise we would experience the past, the future, and all possible pasts and futures simultaneously; experiencing every version of ourselves all at once. There would be no "passage of time" as we experience it normally, and if it could even be said that we were able to 'think' at all in this state, it would be completely alien to our normal experience.

Although each possible outcome is experienced by a version of ourselves, the timeline leading up to each of those versions will, by and large, be internally consistent. Each version of you will remember a consistent history, which allows them to explain *why* they ended up making that choice. If you could look at the Timeless Multiverse from the outside, it would be possible to trace each person's consistent timeline. Everyone considers themselves to have this kind of personal consistency because their own memory makes sense to them. The key to this is the description 'each possible outcome'. Although it is technically possible (for example) for everything in the world to turn into strawberry ice-cream at any moment, there would have to be a previous sequence of events that led to it occurring if we want to have any chance of observing it. It is far more likely for the world of strawberry ice-cream to be a result of, say, a supervillain with a strawberry ice-cream conversion gun, than it would be for the world to spontaneously undergo a strawberry ice-cream quantum fluctuation. And considering that you would have to wait (on average) for longer than the age of the universe just to be able to observe a single molecule in the air spontaneously turn into gold, let alone strawberry ice-cream, I think we can put a certain amount of trust in the macroscopic narratives that we observe in our normal life.

However, even within the set of normal, observable narratives, as we interleave amongst them, constantly changing timelines, the versions of people you meet will not be the same versions you met yesterday, or even a few moments ago! Luckily, because we are all constantly being entangled with our environment (the *decoherence* that I talked about earlier), the limitations imposed on us by that entanglement means that despite navigating our own unique personal path through the multiverse, our experiences tend, on the whole, to mesh with what I refer to as 'The Consensus', and what everyone else would refer to as 'normal life' i.e. everyone else's experiences agree, so that we end up assuming that we are all living in a single universe. Even if the versions of people you met yesterday are not the same versions as those you meet today, they will be sufficiently similar, so as to be consistent with your memories of how they were yesterday. And vice versa - their memories of you will, in most cases, be sufficiently similar that they consider you too, to be the same person they met the day before.

This means that whichever timeline you end up in, whether by normal or by magical means, that timeline will almost always contain versions of everyone who will agree *that is how it is* and furthermore, *that's how it always was*. And vice versa - when you discover that a magician has failed to implement his magic, and you were not involved in the magic, the Consensus is on your side - you have not been included in the set of paths where his magic succeeded. This is also why magic needs to be experienced - any magician who has success after success in their work will end up interacting with more and more different sections of the Consensus. Everyone else, who are outside the magician's path, will, statistically, not interact with the version of the magician that has *all* the successes.

Ironically, quantum decoherence means that we can experience real coherence in our daily lives. Magically, however, the Consensus is like the tar baby that Brer Fox set as a trap for Brer Rabbit, in the Uncle Remus story. The more Brer Rabbit struggled with the tar baby, the more he became stuck to it. It's difficult to break away and choose a different direction when you are entangled with everyone else. I'll talk about this more when we come to the discussion on magical techniques.

Thank you for bearing with me so far. In the next section, we will finally get to the question 'Why is this complete reworking of our view of the universe necessary to understand how magic actually works?'.

The Mechanism of Magic

In the introduction, I talked about "causing change to occur in accordance with one's Will" and how that describes both normal and 'magical' change. In normal change, there are obvious links between cause and effect - you order a meal, pay for it, and, hey presto - the meal arrives! This astounds no-one.

Magical change, however, seems very different. You perform a magical ritual of some kind - which may not have any physical components or even be visible to the naked eye - and sometime later, from a few seconds to a few days, weeks, months or even years, the thing you wanted to achieve (hopefully) occurs.

The Timeless Multiverse model shows us that we perceive our lives as a single sequence of consecutive events because we are incapable of experiencing more than a short section of a single time line at a single time. In reality, our brains are switching from brain state to brain state along huge numbers of time lines like frames in the world's fastest movie, driven by increasing entropy. The ordinary choices we make help decide the paths we end up experiencing.

Magical change is the same; only here, the only difference between the outcomes you experience are the states you put your brain into. You choose your outcome purely by trying to map your mind onto the required series of brain states that leads to you experiencing the desired outcome. Remember; your brain state not only includes a snapshot of your thought processes and your memories (however they are encoded) but also the encoding of sense data from the outside world. Selecting the required series of states may result in hallucination, as you manipulate the encoding of that sense data. Lucid dreaming, where one attempts to manipulate one's dreams by being aware within the dream that one is dreaming, is considered good practice for magicians, as the ability to affect one's internal landscape is good practice for learning to affect the external landscape.

Obviously the remapping that results in actual physical outcomes does not happen at a conscious level, otherwise people would be getting everything they wanted all the time; and what a disaster that would be!

The point is that magic can be considered a variant on normal human consciousness; what programmers refer to as an 'edge case'. What is an edge case? Consider an instruction such as 'follow your dreams'. This seems like a straightforward and uplifting piece of advice until you start to think about some of the dreams you've had. That dream where you had sex with the Prime Minister? Best not follow that one. An edge case is when you discover unexpected behaviour by introducing extreme parameters. In this case, if normal choices result in changes in the path of events we experience, what happens if the only differences between two sets of possible outcomes are the changes that occur in our heads? You could align yourself to one outcome or another purely by altering your state of mind. This is the heart of what magic actually is.

Consider all the possible timelines stretching in front of you into the future. As long as they are in the future from your point of view, they are still coherent, still in superposition until our 'present' wave of decoherence reaches them and they become part of the present (and then the past) for us.

Decoherence is about how fast a path is chosen out of all the possible paths when there is a quantum event. The level at which the decoherence of the paths occurs, to provide us with single outcomes, clearly takes place at a very deep level in the brain (and, as I previously said, at a ridiculously high speed - many powers of ten faster than our brains work). This prevents us from ever being able to experience more than one path at a time. Even the simplest animals will have a variant of our 'single path' experience; if a fly (for example) could see more than one path, spiders would starve to death. The fly would always pick the path where it did not fly into the spider web! In fact, if any animal (including ourselves) could see more than one path, those paths we would never take could not exist. If an outcome exists, there must be a version of the experiencer that experiences that path.

So, again, what is it that allows the magic to happen?

The key to it is entropy. Remember; for any given macroscopic outcome, the more combinations of atoms that can lead to that outcome, the greater the entropy. And with informational entropy, the more predictable the outcome, the less entropy there is.

With both types, entropy can be considered to be a type of ignorance. In 'normal' (thermodynamic) entropy, we ignore the microstates themselves just to get one or more macroscopic facts about them (ignoring the movements of individual molecules to get the temperature of a gas, for example). In informational entropy, the entropy is literally how much we don't know about the future of an event.

At this point, I'd like to introduce a notation that I've found useful in visualising magical events. I call them "outcome cones", although they should probably be more accurately named "entropy cones", since the higher the entropy amongst outcomes, the greater the number of outcomes that are available that could contain your desired outcome.

As you start from a certain point in time, the set of outcomes increase, spreading out from that point in a cone. So I draw a cross-section through that cone; plotting time increase (more properly entropy increase, but still) against number of outcomes, like so:

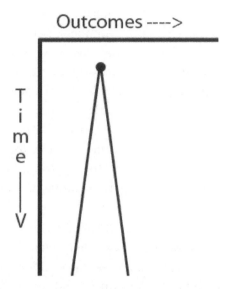

The cross section drawn will usually be restricted, to illustrate a desired set of outcomes. The more outcomes that include the desired set of circumstances, the wider the cone, as we see here in the contrast between A and B.

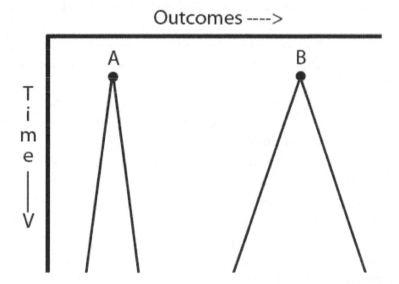

So for the best chance for magic to occur, both thermodynamic and informational entropy need to be maximised. Maximising thermodynamic entropy means increasing the number of possible outcomes that include you experiencing the desired result, usually by stating your desire in such a way as to maximise that number, as shown in the diagram above. I'll talk more about correctly stating your desire in the practical magic section.

Maximising informational entropy means that, out of that list of outcomes from thermodynamic entropy, you need to maximise the outcomes that you magically have access to. Anything you remember will be connected with events that have already decohered in your personal timeline, and you will then have the harder task of finding a result set where, not only does the desired event happen, it must also be a set where you have convinced yourself that your own memory is false! Messing around with your brain in this way is not recommended.

So how to avoid making your magical task even harder than it already is? You need to limit the amount of information you have about the subject of the magical act between the time of that magical act and the time of its conclusion - maximising your ignorance about any possible intermediate steps between the beginning of the magic and its desired result. Otherwise, anything you find out connected with what you've been doing magic about, could end up endangering the successful conclusion of the act.

It's already known from experiment, that on the quantum level, too much observation can literally make change impossible (This is known as the quantum Zeno effect). If an isolated radioactive atom (for example) is constantly measured, that atom will never decay during the period of constant observation; the quantum version of 'a watched pot never boils'. Since the process you are attempting to exploit is so delicate, it is a fine line between avoiding gaining knowledge that will tie your outcomes prematurely, and stumbling around in complete ignorance!

Ideally, the successful conclusion to your magic should hit you 'out of the blue' after successfully putting thoughts of the magic out of your mind. More will be said about this aspect in the section on practical magic.

As we saw in the section on Chaos theory, the human world is subject to complex dynamics and delicate balances. It is this complexity that we need to exploit, both in ourselves and others, to maximise both kinds of entropy: 'scaling events' to maximise thermodynamic entropy, and manipulating our own internal complexity to maximise informational entropy. Modern magicians sometimes refer to this kind of manipulation as 'hacking your brain'.

Retroactive Magic

One of the problems people (and indeed magicians!) have with magic is the idea of magic working retroactively. The kind of scenario I'm talking about is this: Say you are living in Britain; you perform a magical act to receive a physical letter from Australia. The next day, a letter arrives from Australia. Clearly, the letter would have to have been sent long before the magical Act had been performed, and perhaps, even before it had been thought of.

How can such things be? Let's look at it in terms of outcome cones embedded in the larger multiverse.

We begin with two points. A, which is where the magical act is performed, and B, where the letter is actually sent.

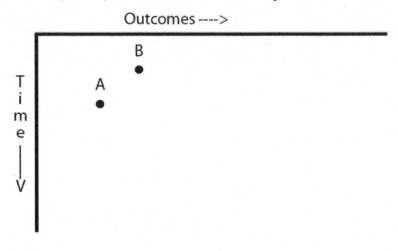

At this point, B does not have to be in any past set of outcomes that has lead to A.

Now we draw the cones.

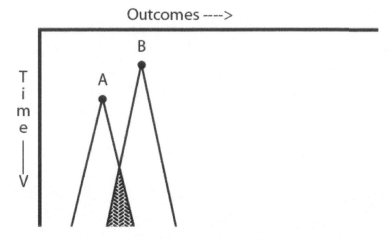

The cone from A is all the outcomes where the magical act was performed. The cone from B is all the outcomes where a letter was sent from Australia.

As you can see, there is an intersection of the two cones, shaded in. This is the set of outcomes where the magical act was performed and a letter was sent from Australia, i.e. the set of outcomes where the Act was successful. Your task is to align yourself with that intersection so that that is what you experience. You will notice that the more time passes, the bigger the intersection - it may even be enough time for the letter to have made its way to you without needing to have been retroactively summoned.

Of course, this diagram also highlights that there is an area containing outcomes where you performed a magical act and no letter arrived! Apart from the fact that the diagram has no scale and no actual measurements, not every magical act will have successful results for every possible outcome. You may just end up in the wrong part of the cone due to the extremely delicate nature of the magical act coupled with the fact that all possible outcomes must occur. You are trying to increase your chances; it is rarely possible to increase them to 100%.

Divination

Another part of what people usually consider magic is divination - looking into the future.

Magicians say "divine short, enchant long". You should only try and predict for a short way into the future, because the further forward you go, the more divergent the futures become - predicting the future of anything other than the simplest, most linear systems becomes impossible after a relatively short time, for the same reasons as we talked about earlier with regard to the weather. When it comes to enchantment/magic/making things happen, as we've seen, the longer you give magic to work when trying to achieve something, the wider the spread of outcomes from the original decision point, and, hopefully, the more chances for you to end up experiencing a successful outcome.

Methods of divination (rune-stones, tarot, etc.) mostly follow similar patterns to each other. You have a selection of objects, each with predetermined meanings. You make a random selection amongst them, and then, after optionally arranging them in a structure, attempt to make a coherent divination from the meanings of each of the selected objects. Or, like the I-Ching, you create a random pattern or patterns from identical things, and then make the divination from the predetermined meanings of the patterns formed.

The difficulty comes when you consider the question "Is the act of predicting something that subsequently occurs actually enchantment?" That is, are you actually magically causing the event that you think you have predicted?

I would say that the answer depends on how much time elapses between the prediction and the event. If the period is, say, less than two weeks (the maximum period for predicting the weather with any accuracy) then the chances are much reduced that enough time has passed to cause the event to happen as a result of your prediction. As we saw with retroactive magic, (which this would be an example of) the two outcome cones (the following timeline of the magical act, and the desired result) need a time period to spread out and intersect, since that intersection is the only place where the magic has been done *and* the correct result obtained. That time period might *start* before a normal result has time to work, but the more time, the more outcomes there will be in the intersection, and thus more chance that you will experience one of the successful ones.

If the period is more than, say, a month, not only is there much more time available for the intersection of act and result, the chances of having *predicted* the resultant path become less and less likely as the outcomes become more and more divergent from your original start point. An accurate prediction becomes less and less interesting the further into the future you go, as the only predictions which will be accurate are the ones with less new information in them. You can predict with a high degree of accuracy that the sun will rise in a year's time, but this is not an interesting prediction. Instead, the further forward in time you go, the more likely your interesting *and* accurate 'predictions' are to have been magically *caused* by you instead.

So (for example) any Tarot readings 'for the year ahead' need to thought of as climate indicators rather than weather predictions.

Parapsychology and Magic

As I mentioned, investigators have been attempting to apply the scientific method to parapsychological phenomena for over a hundred years. Rather than go through the entire history, I'd like to draw your attention to some points that I feel are salient to the Timeless Multiverse.

The first person to set up a laboratory dedicated to investigating parapsychology was Dr. (later Professor) J.B. Rhine. He used packs of specially designed cards to investigate telepathy. Each card had one of the following symbols on one side: a hollow circle, a plus sign, three vertical wavy lines, a hollow square, and a hollow five-pointed star. An experimenter would select a card from a shuffled pack (shuffled by hand to start with and then later by machine), and the subject would attempt to divine which of the five designs it was. The results were (on average out of the eighty-five thousand trials) twenty-eight successes out of a hundred tries; chance would have produced twenty successes out of a hundred. This seemed to show that telepathy was a real, if unreliable, thing.

Then Rhine discovered that the subjects could still successfully divine the card even if the experimenter did not look at it. They could apparently sense concealed objects at a distance, which is usually referred to as clairvoyance. None of the ideas they had about telepathy could possibly apply to this phenomenon.

It gets better. One of the first people to attempt to replicate Rhine's findings, Dr. Soal, experimented with 160 subjects over

128,350 guesses of the five-symbolled cards. He got results no better than chance until a colleague suggested that he look for subjects who guessed the card *before* or *after* the current card. Dr. Soal analysed his results again and found one subject who could consistently guess, not the current card, but the *next* card, with a success rate of twenty-nine instead of the twenty out of a hundred. This subject, Basil Shackleton, was apparently looking into the future *and* reading the mind of the experimenter.

One last set of experiments by Rhine from 1934 were not published until ten years later - the successful influencing of dice, at first rolled by hand, then by electrically driven rotating cages. Since it was assumed that the mind was acting directly on the physical objects, it was known as psychokinesis or telekinesis.

Where the experimenters had been looking to investigate one mysterious phenomenon, they now had four! Telepathy, clairvoyance, precognition, psychokinesis - there was a lot of argument about which of these experiments directly contradicted the known laws of physics. (Or indeed which of them violated physics *the most*.)

What I needed were experiments which acted as closely as possible on quantum level entities; experiments equivalent in scaling to Schrödinger's Cat, where a single atomic event is used as the trigger for a macroscopic event that can easily be seen with the naked eye.

I found a program which was tailor-made to give me some answers.

Robert Jahn was a rocket scientist at Princeton until he became interested in parapsychology. He devised a rigorous series of experiments in the late 1970's (the Princeton Engineering Anomalies Research or 'PEAR' Program) to test whether human beings could affect the output of random number generators. These generators were based on the white noise output of a diode (provable to be quantumly indeterminate), and designed as carefully as possible to be free from innate bias and physical or environmental tampering.

The machine would produce random bits, zero and one, as if they were two sides of a coin, and display them. The results were immediately punched to paper tape and also stored on file.

Although the experiments were rigorously designed, built, and carried out, Jahn also recognised that the results hinged on the states of mind of human beings, and so the experimentation area was made to be comfortable, almost like a living room, with variable lighting, background music, sofas and snacks.

First, the apparatus was left to carry out tens of thousands of trials, with no interference or human presence, to make sure that it had no innate bias. The results from these test runs matched perfectly with chance.

Then, each 'operator' (as Jahn refers to the people taking part in the experiment) would proceed in three different ways - they would do 'runs' or 'blocks' of runs to try to force the display to show results higher than chance (PK+ or psychokinesis+), force it to display results lower than chance (PK- or psychokinesis-), or they would not try to influence the output at all (BL or baseline). Bear in mind that a result deviating sufficiently from chance is still a success, regardless of whether that result is significantly greater than chance, or significantly less than chance. The BL result should allow the experimenters to see if it is just the presence of a person that affects the output, regardless of their intention.

Over the period of the experiment, forty-seven men and women of various ages and backgrounds completed two and a half million trials, generating roughly 670 million bits of data.

The most impressive magical results are gained when they are drawn from the extreme ends of the bell curve, normally as one-off experiences, like Jung's scarab that I mentioned in the introduction. Rhine's experiments showed a 40% increase over chance in eighty-five thousand trials. Shackleton's precognition showed a 45% increase over chance in 3,789 trials.

Professor Jahn's experiments, however, show people still

managing to skew chance over thousands and thousands of trials, where you would normally expect the quantity of those trials to be so great as to hit the average as hard as the unattended calibration runs. And yet the PK+ data exceeds chance by two parts in a thousand, whilst the PK- data exceeds chance by about twice that much. Those are against chance by fifty thousand to one, and a hundred thousand to one.

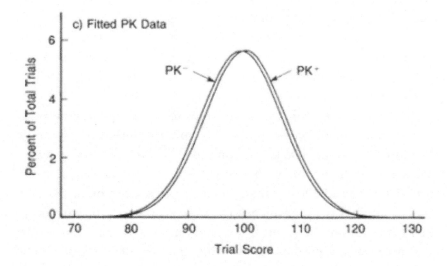

Although this variation away from chance seems minute, it is the huge number of trials that makes it impressive. The more attempts you make, the more likely your total outcomes will veer towards the average (one of the possible explanations for what parapsychology refers to as 'the decline effect' where success in parapsychological experiments often drops off, the longer the experiment goes on for). To be able to steal even a tiny measure from chance over such a large number of attempts shows why magic, this edge case of normal human consciousness, has the potential to be an important agent of change.

Jahn's work follows earlier experiments by Rhine's successor, Helmut Schmidt, who created a device, in this case directly driven by the detection of electrons emitted from Strontium-90 (so just as quantumly indeterministic as Jahn's white noise diode), which would randomly light one of four coloured lamps. The subject's task was to guess which of the lamps would light next - so precognition rather than psychokinesis. Schmidt carried out just over 63,000 trials, and, interestingly, his results gave odds against chance of two thousand million to one - supporting the idea that an increasing number of trials lessens the significance of the result.

So, what do these 'psychic powers' have in common, both with each other, and with the Timeless Multiverse? The answer is *correlation*. Just as with the entangled particles and their non-locality that we looked at in quantum physics, no useful information has been exchanged until one person knows the information from both the source and the destination - and of course, that requires that information to be transmitted by normal means, which will be slower than the speed of light, and thus not breaking the laws of physics.

With telepathy/clairvoyance/precognition, the result requires the person's guess to be correlated with the card that was in question, otherwise how would you know that the guess was correct? The probabilistic (read: unreliable) nature of these experiments mean that you cannot know the results without this correlation, even if it takes place a few seconds or a few years after the event. So, unfortunately, telepathy is no use as the kind of 'mental radio' that science fiction is so fond of, since without sender and receiver comparing notes in a normal fashion, you have no way of knowing whether the message sent matches the message received. (And in fact, several parapsychological studies where there was never any feedback showed only chance results.)

Psychokinesis is slightly different - this is actual magic; engineering coincidence so that the desired result manifests. There still needs to be correlation, though - the experimenter doing the measuring needs to end up in the same result set as the successful subject.

So we now know what magic is and how it manifests. So how do we apply it, and what techniques do we use?

Belief

Earlier, I talked about how magic happens at a level in the brain below the conscious mind. How does the interface work, between our minds (viewable as a kind of software 'running' on the hardware of our brains) and the physical process of decoherence (which ensures that we only remember a single sequence of events)?

As an aside, the idea of 'mind as software' also helps shed light on why the mind is so difficult to analyse and understand. As an experiment, a bunch of computer scientists tried to deduce the software running on a computer purely by measuring the electrical signals of the CPU, as if they were neurologists and the CPU was a brain. Despite knowing the exact wiring of the entire CPU, and being able to measure each of the signals without error, it proved impossible to deduce the nature of the software design; measuring the signals, no matter how precisely, does not help you to play Donkey Kong. And of course the brain is many, many times more complex than a CPU.

Beliefs are aspects of your consciousness that interface with your subconscious; they are the lowest level of your consciousness that you have direct access to. It is by manipulating these aspects of consciousness that we attempt to do magic.

Belief is something that you end up assuming without conscious thought. A good rule of thumb to judge depth of belief, is when your beliefs are challenged; how much emotion do you experience whilst trying to defend them? Someone asks you why you should think something so stupid, and you feel a surge of anger flood through you. Whether you are right or wrong, it's a sure sign that this belief is pretty deep-rooted.

Magic requires a belief system to implement it, but it's unimportant what that belief system consists of; you just have to believe it. The simplest belief system for doing magic is a belief in your own abilities as a magician. More complex belief systems manifest as things like magical 'systems', religions, or even things like homoeopathy.

Homoeopaths believe in a kind of 'sympathetic magic', that 'like cures like', choosing a substance that would cause the patient's symptoms in a healthy person, and then diluting it until there will be no molecules of that substance left in the solution, believing that the process of dilution actually makes the 'medicine' stronger. It's a perfect example of how what the practitioners think of as a 'theory' or a 'model' is actually a very complex (and expensive!) belief system. The complexity of the system (e.g. at each iteration of dilution, the vessel with the solution is shaken vigorously to 'activate the vital energy' of the substance) adds to its gravitas for the believers, making them more likely to believe it, although generations of experimenters on the placebo effect know that a simple sugar pill is just as effective. Fabulous results can of course be achieved with the placebo effect, but magic is not a thing to be relied on constantly. You should always have a Plan A, or, as it's normally referred to in this area, medicine. There is no reason why the belief involved in the placebo effect cannot be deployed just as effectively when taking the actual medicine. You don't have to invent extra belief in the drug when it's already been proven to do the job.

So, no matter how complicated and involved the belief system, it is purely a tool - like a chisel, a pair of tweezers, or a computer. You can teach yourself to believe something just as you can teach yourself to ride a bike; practising until you no longer have to consciously think about it. This 'autopilot' in the brain is something we are very familiar with - you might notice that if you start actively thinking about riding the bike after you have learned, the process of riding suddenly becomes more difficult as you become aware of what you're doing! The brain's 'autopilot' is very useful for riding a bike or playing tennis, but it is possible to give it too much power.

This is because the autopilot is controlled by a very deep part of the brain called the striatum, which is involved in putting rewarding plans into action; coordinating the way our decisions and behaviours add up to a feeling of pleasure. When we first develop a habit, the prefrontal cortex (where it's generally agreed our conscious thinking gets done) is involved in the formation of the habit, but if we repeat the habit enough times, the prefrontal cortex no longer activates, leaving only the reward/action parts of the loop. This is supposed to be so that our mind is free to plan other things, and is fine for riding a bike, but not so fine for other things.

As Colin Wilson, the occult researcher, put it: "The first time you listen to the song, you listen to it. The twentieth time, if you're not careful, the robot listens to it for you."

Programming this autopilot mechanism with appropriate beliefs is what we are going to use to do magic. This includes techniques to suppress the conscious mind, so that, like riding the bike, we don't interfere with the autopilot.

So how do you teach yourself to believe? You can do it by something akin to method acting. You could, for example, create a character who believes the belief system you require, for the duration that you require it, then teach yourself to inhabit that character. "Fake it 'till you make it" as jazz musicians say. The general wisdom is that you should choose a belief system that meshes best with the kind of magical act that you are trying to achieve, to make it easier for you to convince yourself. You might, for example, decide that you are fighting against something with this magic, so Mars, the god of War, would be a suitable character to invoke. Or if love is the focus of your magic, then the goddess Venus might well be a suitable vehicle for it. This aspect of your magic is limited only by your creativity.

It is also extremely important that you banish this character after the work has been completed - just like method actors, the character you have created can interfere with your life or even overtake you, and you need to banish it in order to make sure that you are yourself again.

As an example of this kind of banishing, you could wear a costume which you associate only with the character. Then you can banish the character by disposing of the costume, possibly with a ritual. You absolutely need to impress upon yourself that you are no longer that character. Grant Morrison, comic writer and magician: "Banishing reminds you that no matter how many gods you talk to, no matter how many fluorescent realms you visit, you still have to come home, take a shit, be able to cook dinner, water the plants and, most importantly, talk to people without scaring them."

Magic is the practical heart of religion. Most religions consist of two parts: a moral code (don't kill people, don't sleep with your sister etc.), and then instructions and rituals for "making things happen". Praying for a good harvest, praying for victory in battle etc. This "making things happen" is obviously magical; how we attempt to affect outcomes by non-normal means.

Consider the ability to do magic (or "the power of faith" as you might call it in a religious sense) as the elephant in the Jainist parable of the blind men and the elephant. Each blind man grasps a different part of the elephant and declares that he knows what the elephant is like. The one who grasps the trunk declares that the elephant is like a snake, the one who grasps the leg declares that the elephant is like a tree, and so on. Because the underlying mechanism of magic is not known, people often mistake the belief system they are using for the thing itself, or, as scholar Alfred Korzybski put it, "the map is not the territory".

Thus, these belief systems, and all their components are actually part of the map and not part of the territory. For homoeopathy, these components are the 'drugs' they sell, whilst for religions, they include the God or gods.

Many religions declare that "theirs is the only truth" - to make their belief system more convincing, both to themselves and to anyone they are trying to persuade to join them. What use would be a belief system that isn't convincing enough to believe in?

There is a sociological theorem called 'the Thomas Theorem' (since it was postulated by two sociologists called William Isaac Thomas and Dorothy Swaine Thomas) and it states that 'If men define situations as real, they are real in their consequences.' This leads to the disturbing conclusion that although a particular thing is not real, the *idea* of that thing becomes a real thing; a thing can be real, even if it does not exist!

For example: the horror writer H.P. Lovecraft wrote about an evil book called 'The Necronomicon' which contained great magic powers, but unfortunately turned most of the characters that read it, insane. He was later shocked and surprised when people started writing to him, asking where they could find a copy! In the end, he had to write a short essay about the book, emphasising that it did not exist, he really had just made it up, and that to the best of his knowledge there was no such book! And yet there are several (real) books, all purporting (with varying degrees of seriousness) to be the actual Necronomicon. Several libraries have spoof entries for the Necronomicon in their catalogues (perhaps marked as permanently 'out on loan'). The idea of this completely non-existent book has taken on a life of its own!

A second example, and one that might surprise you: Money. If you take a British five pound note, and peer very carefully underneath where it says "Bank of England", there is a sentence in tiny letters: "I PROMISE TO PAY THE BEARER ON DEMAND THE SUM OF FIVE POUNDS." This tells us that British banknotes are really a kind of IOU. Originally, we would barter with each other for items - I have some apples, you have some wool, we do a swap and everyone is happy. What if all you have is apples, though? How do you barter with people who don't want apples? You would have to find a third person who wants apples and will swap them for a third thing that *is* wanted, so you can then go on and swap for the thing you wanted in the first place. To prevent this problem, we find a thing to trade for, that everyone values. I can then trade my apples for this new thing, and trade it to anyone else for whatever I want. Originally it was things like gold and silver that everyone recognises as valuable. This is what the five pound note is promising to pay you on demand. The gold and silver, though, is only the representation of the labour we expended to produce the things (like apples) that we use to trade. Then the five pound notes (and every other currency) are only the representation of *that*. The money only works because we all believe it to be real, otherwise it would just be so much confetti.

In Zen Buddhism, when talking about reality, they say "First there is a mountain. Then there is no mountain. Then there is." In other words, it is useful to see things as being real, then to look on a deeper level, and see them to be unreal, then finally look even deeper and see how they *are* real.

You represent your magical desire with a sigil, an object, or perhaps a ritual act, to associate the magic with some kind of real external thing. The purpose of this is to make it more 'real' to ourselves, strengthening our belief system. If you become utterly convinced that gods and/or spirits are real, it will come as no surprise to you when they are swayed by your pleas and do your bidding. Thus, gods and spirits can be very real, even if they do not, in fact, exist. It is common for magicians to create simple 'mindforms' or 'servitors' for specific purposes such as bringing money, sending a message etc. Just the act of convincing yourself that the thing is real, makes it more real, as you then begin to act on the consequences of its 'reality'. In this case, of course, the consequences are magical in nature.

Both magicians and parapsychologists have experimented with this ability to create real things that do not exist. A group of parapsychologists in 1972 invented a fictional historical figure called 'Philip Aylesford'. They gave him a brief but exciting life story, and even created a portrait of him. Once everyone taking part had fixed 'Philip' in their minds, they attempted to contact him via a seance. And Philip replied to them. They asked him questions and he replied by rapping the table, despite the fact that everyone there knew that they had invented him.

A group of magicians, more than thirty years later, went an impressive step further; they created a goddess. The goddess in question was Apophenia (and her mad twin sister Pareidolia). Apophenia is the ability to see meaningful patterns in things where most people do not, and is considered a very good thing to be able to do as a magician. If you can see patterns that connect disparate things, you forge a connection in your mind between those things - hopefully a deep enough one to allow a desired outcome to be unconsciously represented by one of the connected things. Pareidolia, on the other hand, is the distraction of seeing random patterns in things. As Peter Carroll, one of the magicians who created the goddess(es) put it:

"I concluded that whilst Apophenia could bring the Universe in a grain of sand to our attention, Pareidolia merely distracts us with the face of the Virgin Mary in a pavement pizza."

A servitor that helps you find loose change behind the sofa is one thing, but a goddess should be treated much more seriously. Again, thanks to the nature of belief, the degree of seriousness with which you treat your creations will dictate how powerful and influential over you they become. As H.P. Lovecraft says in 'The Case of Charles Dexter Ward': "Do not call up that which you cannot put down".

There is a stage in every magician's development which Aleister Crowley called 'crossing the Abyss'. The writer and philosopher Robert Anton Wilson ("I don't have any beliefs but I have a lot of suspicions") called it 'navigating Chapel Perilous'. You, the magician, have spent time struggling with magic and finally it really works. You've experienced something that is completely at odds with the way you thought of reality up until that point. This is where the Abyss/Chapel Perilous opens up in front of you. There are basically three ways of dealing with it. Some people will just deny the new experience; shutting the door and not opening it again because they can't deal with the changes to themselves that the new experiences require. Others become convinced that this power makes them Masters of the Universe; they enter and never leave, lost in their own belief system as they mistake the map for the territory, whilst giving themselves over to varying degrees of self-delusion. If you are to succeed as a magician, you must take the third way, and pass *through* the Abyss/Chapel Perilous; this corresponds to the willingness to incorporate the seemingly contradictory experiences of magic into your worldview without being overtaken or overwhelmed by it.

PART 2: Practical Magic

Introduction to Practical Magic

I mentioned in the introduction that without an actual theory, magic has been, for hundreds of years, a practical matter of trial and error. For example, if you do a ritual to help the sun rise every morning, how do you know whether it is actually your rituals that cause the sun to rise every morning? And if you thought it was, how much courage would you need to test it by *not* performing the ritual and thus taking the risk of the sun not coming up?

Joking aside, without a theory (read: explanation), how can you work out which behaviours in your rituals are necessary and which are superfluous? And even then, *why* are they necessary?

In this section, I'll introduce you to the way that magic is done in a practical sense and attempt to explain what each aspect can contribute to a magical act becoming a success. I've attempted to strip the magical experience down to the bare minimum so that I don't start becoming someone who mistakes the map for the territory.

Remember: these techniques for practical magic are the concentrated essence of thousands of years of "magical cathedral building" - trial and error showing us how to build magic that 'stays up'. Now that the first section of the book has given you a basic theory of magic, I'm now going to use this theory to explain *why* these techniques work.

The Smallest Piece of Magic

Before we get stuck into the details of magical techniques, perhaps it's time I got you to actually do some magic. We'll start with literally the smallest piece of magic that you can do.

This is a Necker Cube.

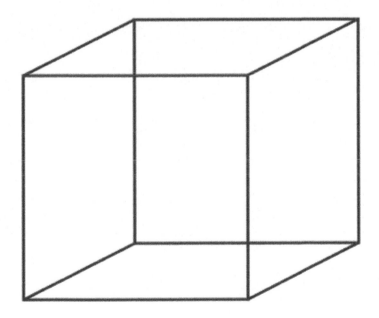

It's normally described as an optical illusion. Because it has no depth cues, your brain will see it first from one direction and then from another, seemingly randomly. Your magical task is to choose one of the possible orientations and see the cube in that orientation, holding it for fifteen to twenty seconds - or even longer if you can! By doing this, you have altered your physical perception by force of will. Or in terms of the Timeless Multiverse, you have chosen a particular path in your timeline, purely by wilfully altering your brain state.

Like I said, literally the smallest piece of magic that you can do - one with no external results, but one where you can see the results immediately - although it may surprise you how difficult it is!

So, let's look now at the general techniques of practical magic - in the hope of producing results much more ambitious than the Necker Cube!

Practical Magic: Techniques

"The Secret is not a secret. You could state it to the world in the plainest language imaginable and it would still be a secret."

Magic is still considered a secret, even today when magicians are not persecuted as they were in the past.

It is a secret because it relies on experience. It belongs to a class of things that, ultimately, cannot merely be described, they need to be experienced.

'Occult' means 'hidden' - not hidden as a secret, but hidden as a consequence of the requirement that it be experienced. If you tried to explain what sex was like to someone who had never had sex, you would be very surprised if they turned round to you and declared that they thought you were making it all up! However, this is exactly what happens with magic. Those who are most ready to deny it have not experienced it. I can show you *how* to experience it, but ultimately, no-one can do it for you - the path you follow, you need to follow for yourself, since the line through the multiverse that represents your life is unique to each version of you.

As the existence of this book attests, I am more of a theoretical magician than a practical magician. However, you can't really be a magician without doing any magic! At the beginning of 'Jonathon Strange & Mr. Norrell' by Susanna Clarke, Mr. Norrell pours scorn on the 'Society of English Magic' because all they do is sit and talk about magic; considering it vulgar to actually *do* any.

Firstly, what does doing magic actually feel like? How do you know when you've done it? I believe a short digression can shed some light on the experience. In the late 1960's, an eminent neurophysiologist, Dr. William Grey Walter, performed an experiment where he hooked up electrodes to measure brain activity in his subject's frontal cortex.

When we decide to do something (pick up a glass, press a button, etc.), about half a second before we decide to do it, there is a surge of about twenty microvolts in a large area of the cortex; this surge is known as the 'readiness potential'. This observation in itself has caused a lot of arguments about free will - how can you start doing something before you've decided to do it?

Dr. Walter was, however, not a philosopher. He wanted to see if the readiness potential could be put to some use. He amplified the readiness potential, and when it was detected, he used it to instantly trigger images to appear on a TV screen. The subject, meanwhile, was told that they could bring up images on the screen by pressing a button. The practical upshot of which, was that the images would appear on the screen about half a second *before* the button was pressed. You could describe this as pseudo-psychokinesis. Popular Science magazine called it 'The Wish-Switch'.

For the person doing it, it is a peculiar and novel experience (a couple of the subjects wet themselves slightly in stress or excitement). Firstly, they have to really *want* the event to occur, but if they concentrate on the wanting, instead of on the event itself, the readiness potential does not occur, and thus the 'magical event' does not happen.

The most interesting part for me is the state of mind the subjects described whilst raising the readiness potential. They only succeeded if they were in a state described as "a paradoxical compound of detachment and excitement" which is exactly the feeling I have experienced whilst doing magic successfully. My own, very similar, description was "excitement coupled with a kind of looking away".

This implies to me that, at the root of it, the method of thinking that triggers magical action and the method of thinking that triggers normal action are very similar.

As Dr. Grey himself said: "It's like riding a bicycle. You certainly can't learn how to do it from a book or by being told how. And after you have learned to do it, you still can't explain how you learned. It's simply a part of your knowledge."

Whenever I have done magic, when the coincidences I have engineered become apparent, they are usually surrounded by other coincidences, ones I didn't specifically desire for, in the way that throwing a stone into a pond causes a spreading pattern of ripples. This idea was first brought to my attention in Arthur Koestler's book, 'The Roots of Coincidence', before I had consciously performed any magic myself. He found that the more he researched about coincidence, the more coincidences happened to him, to the point where instead of searching for desired information, he would start to expect that he would 'stumble upon' what he was looking for; books would fall open at the exact page, he would find the book he was looking for in a completely unexpected place. He called this the 'library angel'. I believe this kind of thing to be a surefire sign that you have engineered coincidence, providing useful signs that your magic has had an effect on the timeline you have ended up in - hopefully, from your point of view, a successful one.

For example, after performing one particular (successful) magical act, I discovered the next day that Osama bin Laden had been killed at almost exactly the same time as my magic had successfully concluded. This does not, of course, mean that I *caused* Osama bin Laden to get killed! It shows that while you are attempting to achieve something magically, other things in the multiverse, full as it is of possible outcomes, are up for grabs. Everything that is not specifically included in your magic, and that you are ignorant of, is in flux. Again, you cannot think that you are changing the Universe - you are moving to the place where it is changed; i.e. you are attempting to select from the mind-bogglingly large number of already existing paths that, for you, lie in the future. Your task is to select with regard to a very small aspect of that future; the remainder of the successful result set can be anything that is compatible with both your success, and of course your memories.

As we discussed earlier, magic consists of using belief systems and the mechanism of belief to harness your internal autopilot. Your aim is to use this mechanism, instead of using it to, say, ride a bike, you will be using it to program the 'operating system' level of your brain to navigate towards a desired result over time. Since you have no direct way of accessing this level with your conscious mind, the process to end up on a path containing the outcome you wanted to occur takes place at this very deep level of your brain.

Incidentally, this means that this process is happening randomly all the time, based on the contents of your subconscious. Most of the time, it is cancelled out by the Consensus, but occasionally it will surface in the form of synchronicity. No conscious magical act was performed, but a desire existed deep in the subconscious, and there was a magical result, like Jung and the scarab. Jung wanted to be able to progress his patient's treatment, and his frustration was clearly at a deep enough level to allow the solution to his problem to appear. Obviously, the randomness of which subconscious aspect manifests means the majority of synchronicities will be unlikely, but not necessarily terribly 'meaningful'.

A classic example of this is the French poet Emile Deschamps, who as a child was given plum-pudding (almost unknown in France at that time) by a Monsieur de Fortgibu. Ten years later, he was passing a restaurant and spotted a plum pudding inside. He went inside, only to be told that the pudding had already been bought - by Monsieur de Fortgibu, who kindly shared it with him. Years later again, he went to dinner where a real English plum pudding was to be served. He joked with the hostess that the only thing missing was Monsieur de Fortgibu. At that moment, Monsieur de Fortgibu was announced. He had not been invited; he was very old and senile, and had come to the wrong house by mistake.

So, the aim is to exploit this subconscious mechanism, but use it to produce results that are actually useful.

The process of programming your subconscious is simultaneously very simple and very difficult. The techniques themselves are simple; the way you implement them can be as complex as you like. One of the difficulties lies in making yourself believe the crucial desire instead of thinking about the belief, in the same way as Dr. Walter's experiments required concentration on the desired event and not on the desire itself. The other is the constant entanglement with others (The Consensus) that may drag you away from the result set you want, as if you were a small boat being buffeted by the currents in a fast-flowing river.

As promised, I will strip the techniques down to the barest bones in the hope of making things clearer. The basic steps go like this:

1) Create a statement of your desire.
2) Find something to represent your statement of desire.
3) Bring the representation into your subconscious
4) Try to give the whole thing no further thought.

Let's look at these in turn.

Create a statement of your desire

This is the most important part. It forces you to state what you want as clearly as possible. You need to think of it almost like programming a computer. There must be no ambiguity: and yet, at the same time, it must correctly state your desire whilst leaving as open as possible the method by which that desire might be fulfilled.

For example, if you say "I want to be a great actor" then your desire is already fulfilled; you already *want* to be a great actor.

A better statement would be:

"I WILL be a great actor"

You need to think like the people given three wishes in the old tales. The genie has latitude to interpret your wishes anyway he can. At the same time, you need to avoid being too specific to maximise your chances of success. Willing yourself to, for example, start a relationship with a specific person reduces the number of paths which contain success - and you may find that the version of that person you are capable of being in a relationship with, may not be the person you expected, or were looking for. The result is all you are attempting to specify - this gives you no positive control over the intermediate outcomes that lead to that result.

Desiring instead for someone *like* that person gives you a wider choice of possible success paths.

So, looking at the set of outcomes where you meet someone

called Dave (set A), versus the set where you meet someone called Dave *or* someone called June (set B):

Outcomes ---->

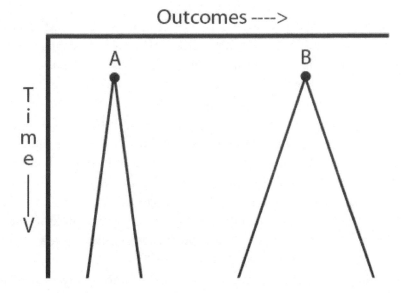

This is attempting to maximise the number of possible paths available - the thermodynamic entropy (although you should probably set your sights higher than just the person's name!). You should also state the desire in such a way as to encompass as many solutions that you currently have no knowledge of. This allows you to maximise the informational entropy - the desired result should not aim to contradict things that you remember having already happened. As I mentioned earlier, the desired result should be consistent with your current memory because otherwise a successful result will make you doubt your own memories.

The last caveat I want to mention is a story called "The Monkey's Paw" by W.W. Jacobs.

A family welcome an old friend returning from travelling the world. With him, he brings a mummified monkey's paw that he claims will grant each owner three wishes.

The father is persuaded by his family to wish for £100. The next day, the manager of the factory his son works at, turns up to break the news that their son has been killed, falling into the factory machinery. He offers the Father money not to bring legal action. Of course, the amount he offers is £100.

"Be careful what you wish for - you might get it" is the lesson here. The universe doesn't care how your desire gets implemented. The chances are, you will get exactly what you ask for, since that was what the process 'had to go on'. You should also avoid wishing for the negation of things. In the same way as 'not thinking of a thing' can easily end up as 'thinking of a thing', wishing for a negation ('I don't want to get ill') can easily end up as the thing itself ('I want to get ill'), especially if you focus on the negative outcome (seeing yourself ill in bed etc.). Instead, focus on a positive statement ('I want to stay healthy') - this is why 'New Age' type magic talks about 'positive thinking' and 'affirmations'. It appears to be the verb that is important, and not any modifiers you might apply to it.

At this point, a short word about cancer. Cancer is caused by a multitude of different factors, the largest of which is random mutation (most of the rest involves cell damage caused by such things as smoking). The programming in a single cell goes awry, and that cell begins to multiply out of control. It is, luckily, unlikely to be caused by just a single mutation (you undergo an average of four random mutations every time you go out in the sun), and, also luckily, our DNA is so full of leftover junk that any one mutation is unlikely to hit the right combination of changes to cause it anyway. The fact remains, however, that a 'successful' cancer is a scaling event *par excellence* (from single cell to life-endangering tumour), so it is a good idea to include a protection ritual of some kind (perhaps something along the lines of 'firstly, do no harm') in any magic you perform, since, as we discussed earlier, the ripples of other coincidences tend to gather around the actual engineered coincidence, and are, by their nature, unpredictable. Taking precautions to try and avoid these kind of unpredictable consequences is only sensible for the magician.

In fact, this is almost certainly the origin of the idea of

beginning any magical ritual with a protection ritual. When you attempt to manipulate coincidence, you are not risking being assailed by demons or spirits, but by these unforeseen side effects, these *other* coincidences. They might easily manifest to you as the work of demons or spirits (depending on whether the belief system you use depends on demons or spirits), but it is really the backlash from your magical work.

Find something to represent your statement of desire

Since the aim of magic is to forge a link between your magical desire and your subconscious, you need some "misdirection". If you think too much about the desired magical act, your conscious mind interferes with the success rate of the magical process, most often by overlaying your actual desire with the desire "I hope this works", thus short-circuiting the act.

Therefore, you should use a representation of the desire. This representation should have only an indirect connection with the desire. This can be achieved in countless ways. 'Sympathetic magic' (for example) says that like goes with like, so considering two things to be alike forms the link between them; one being the desire, and the other being the representation.

This could be a lock of a person's hair, or for more abstract concepts, things such as tables of correspondences, Kabbalah, or other ways of linking real things to such symbols.

A simple example is 'sigil magic'.

Firstly, you express your carefully constructed desire, as clearly as you can, in a sentence.

I WILL BE A GREAT ACTOR

Then you cross out all the vowels and any repeated letters.

W L B   GR T C

Then, from the remaining letters, you create a 'sigil'. There are no hard and fast rules for doing this, but the less the result bears to the original, the better. The best sigils look like magical signs, since that is exactly what they are. Something like this:

You can always simplify it down or redesign it if you don't like it; the important part is that you have *abstracted* your desire. The more you consider this representation of your desire to be external, the less likely you are to interfere with it, and the more likely you are to be able to believe in it. I say again; this sigil method is only one example. The external abstraction of your desire can be literally anything you devise, as long as you forge that strong link between it and your stated desire.

Perhaps the act of popping a balloon might represent the destruction of an obstacle from your life.

Maybe a carefully designed ritual of chanting, with music, coloured lights, scented candles, and stroking of furry seat covers will activate all your senses to impress the desire more deeply upon you.

In fact, since the goal is to plunge your desired outcome as deeply as possible into your subconscious, the greater the number of links you can include to your current beliefs, the better. This is one of the reasons why magicians create or use extensive magical systems - the more deeply embedded the elements of the system (over long practice), the more strongly believed (and thus programmed) any desire expressed in that system will be.

Once you have decided on the symbolising of your desire and produced it, you can move on to the next phase; actually programming it into you.

Bring the representation into your subconscious

Earlier, I explained that the success of magic is partially governed by the things you *don't* know. In front of you, you have the representation of your desire, be it a sigil or a thing or even an action. The important thing is that you have forged a link between this external representation and your (previously clearly stated) desire. Now you need to program it into your subconscious, and for that, it needs to be the only thing in your mind whilst your consciousness is temporarily held in abeyance. This is usually referred to as 'gnosis' (instinctive knowledge), and is used both to reach a lower level of your mind than would normally be available, and to avoid your magical experience being 'I hope this works' instead of the actual desire that you have carefully fashioned.

"But I'm conscious all the time unless I'm asleep!" you say. Luckily for us, this is not actually true. If, for example, you lift two weights and try and judge which is heavier, you will feel the weights, their textures, any irregularities. So while you are conscious of all these things, are you also conscious of the process that decides which one is heavier? Or do you just know which one is heavier without actually thinking about it?

This sounds like another paradox; how can you think of something whilst not thinking of anything?

There are two basic answers to this: you can either clear your conscious mind or overload it. Clearing it usually means meditation; long hours of practice every day until you can still the constant voice in the head that we call 'I'. Of course, there are other benefits to meditation (stress relief etc.), but its main difficulty is correctly described by Aleister Crowley:

"If we sit down quietly and investigate the contents of our minds, we shall find that even at the best of times the principal characteristics are wandering and distraction."

So perhaps overloading the brain is the way to go. The frenzied dancing and drumming of stereotypical Voudun ceremonies do this. The conscious mind is completely submerged in the moment, leaving the way open for the desired magical experience of possession.

On a more personal level, there is what comic writer and magician Grant Morrison calls 'the Wank Method'. At the moment of orgasm, being overwhelmed turns suddenly to emptiness, and this is the perfect moment to expose yourself to the representation of your desire that you created earlier, as your conscious mind is briefly shoved out of the way.

Morrison suggests, amongst other things, writing the symbol on a Post-It note and sticking it to your hand, chest, mirror, or even your partner's forehead.

On the occasions when it's been possible to measure brain activity during magical or paranormal acts, success is associated with suppression of cortical activity; that is, the conscious mind is disengaged at the crucial moment. This is your aim; suppress your consciousness and temporarily replace it with the representation of your desire.

After plenty of experience, you may be able to replace a method of gnosis with a particular attitude of mind, such as Dr. Walter describes in his wish-switching experiments, but this is still difficult to achieve, and, like everything else in magic, needs first to be directly experienced before you can understand how to do it on command.

Now we come to the last part of the magical act; what happens afterwards?

Try to give the whole thing no further thought

So, you have formulated your desire, created your representation of that desire, and burned it into your subconscious. Your magical act is complete. Except it isn't. You are still capable of affecting the outcome right up until the moment you find out whether it has, or hasn't, worked. The magical act is only complete when it is resolved.

Thus, the best thing you can do now is pretend to yourself that nothing ever happened. This way, you attempt to minimise any negative interference from your own mind before the magical act completes.

There is an old joke that says your hiccups will be cured if you can run round the house three times without thinking of the word 'wolf'. The joke being, of course, that thinking about 'not thinking about a thing' is still thinking about that thing.

However, as a magician, this is one of the talents that you require. You need to be able to *actually* not think about the word 'wolf'. Controlling your conscious mind in this way allows you to reduce the self-defeating 'I hope it works'-type interference with your desired set of outcomes. This does mean, however, that you have to balance the importance of the magic (you wouldn't be doing magic if the result wasn't important) which can lead you to keep thinking about it, and the disinterested mindset that minimising the interference requires. Again, long experience can train you to have an unshakable belief in your belief, so that it manifests at a conscious as well as an unconscious level, but in the meantime, you should learn to be able to 'not think about the thing'.

It may well be that when religious people are told to 'have faith', this is an attempt to maximise informational entropy by keeping the subject out of your thoughts. 'Leaving it in the hands of God' being shorthand for the mental trick of not thinking about it.

A corollary to this need to put the magic out of your mind, is the circumstances under which you perform the magic. As we've seen, the process is quite delicate, and everyone who is aware of the magic being done, before it completes, is capable of subconsciously interfering with the process. You will be entangled with them in this matter. This is the other reason why magic is regarded as a secret. Books on the occult are very hit and miss (aside from their value as art), but occasionally you find useful things, even if the magicians do not necessarily know *why* they are useful. Magicians perform magic either alone, or in groups where a lot of trouble is taken (via mood, dress, ritual etc.) to make sure everyone is in the same state of mind, with the purpose of ending up in the same results set. Grimoires warn their readers to keep the spells they contain secret, because just telling someone about them could cause them to lose their power - probably because the time you would be most likely to tell someone about the spell would be the time you were actually trying to use it.

By telling someone who is not involved about your magical act, you are then involving them in that magical act, and they are unlikely to provide a positive contribution; most likely they will muddy the waters even more than usual - you are entangling your world line even more strongly with theirs. For the result to be successful, it now has to include everyone you told, every step of the way.

Of course, it is possible to perform magic in the presence of others - as long as they have no idea you are doing it!

PART 3: Speculations

About Speculation

It may seem to you that I've done enough speculating already throughout this book, but most of the things I've talked about up to this point are anchored pretty firmly in known science (even though it may not seem like it!). Now, however, I'd like to really rev up into the ether and speculate about possible consequences of the Timeless Multiverse and the way we experience it, along with the edge condition of consciousness that we've been referring to as 'magic'.

Is there such a thing as free will?

Is it possible to experimentally investigate the Timeless Multiverse?

What happens during near-death experiences?

What is dark matter?

Where do babies come from?

That last one is more like 'how can magic help make babies?' but I'm still not sure whether that's the best way to put it either...

Free Will

One of the biggest questions about the Timeless Multiverse (for philosophers, at least) is free will. As we saw, General Relativity, by itself, negates the possibility of free will; all we would have would be the ignorance of our predetermined fate as we slog through our lives in the single block Universe. Under the Timeless Multiverse model, however, although all outcomes are predetermined, the path each of us takes through those outcomes is not. So, at the very least, the Timeless Multiverse model removes a whole class of restrictions on free will; it is not a proof of free will, but free will is not incompatible with it. Interestingly, philosophers talk about 'compatibilism' which is the idea that free will and determinism are compatible. Unfortunately, their definition of determinism in this discussion says that only one future can be possible at any one time, which puts their whole discussion out of joint with the Timeless Multiverse model. Our determinism is not their determinism.

On the one hand, it can be argued that our choices in life allow us to experience a set of consequences compatible with those choices, and that if we had chosen differently, we would experience a different set of consequences. This is a reasonable definition of free will: could we have chosen differently? On the other hand, since every single possible outcome is represented at all points in the multiverse, that implies that our power of choice is still illusory, since switching between random choices, even if we are in ignorance of the consequences of those choices, does not necessarily count as free will.

I would argue that at the macroscopic level, the path we end up experiencing needs to have a narrative. Because it is extremely unlikely that our normal run of experiences will suddenly be disrupted by, say, the world turning into strawberry ice-cream in the way that I mentioned earlier, we expect our actions, by and large, to have logical outcomes. The fact that we normally experience a logical, explicable sequence implies that the only paths that exist on the main track are those with these kind of histories. It's all very well imagining that at every moment there are sprays of dead-end universes branching off, where everyone explodes or turns into strawberry ice-cream, but it's easy to forget how mind-bogglingly unlikely it is that any of us should ever experience such a thing - any outcome that appears to violate the usual classical laws of physics (especially on such a large scale) would take many, many lifetimes of the known universe to occur spontaneously.

So the outcomes we experience will almost certainly be limited to the choices we experience at any moment, coupled with the variations of the environment. There may be (for example) outcomes where Hitler shot himself in 1914, and other outcomes where a piano fell on his head. We would, however, expect there to be a narrative sequence of events that led to those outcomes, and not for Hitler to just spontaneously shoot himself, or for him to stand around in the street waiting for falling pianos! These kind of bizarre outcomes are still massively more likely than Hitler turning into strawberry ice-cream, but they should still be considered as making up a very tiny percentage of the outcomes from any particular point.

As we saw when learning about entropy, there is not just a single path for each choice. At any given point, the number of outcomes of a single macroscopic choice will be split between how likely each of the different choices are. So, if the choice is between three different flavours of ice-cream, and you like them all equally, roughly 1/3 of the outcomes will be allocated to each flavour. Whichever choice you make must correspond with an actual outcome. You can consider this to be a form of free will; if you had chosen otherwise, you would just be following a different path instead.

Again; all the paths are deterministic; which outcomes we end up experiencing are not - but each set of outcomes will include, in its past, the choices you made to reach that set of outcomes.

Frauchiger-Renner and the Consensus

When I talked earlier about the Consensus, I mentioned that entanglement and decoherence working together, conspire to produce the illusory perspective that we all live in the same, single, Universe. Is it possible though, just as the double-slit experiment reveals the quantum world to us, there could be an experiment which tests and reveals the nature of the Consensus to us?

It may be that such an experiment has already been thought of - it's called the Frauchiger-Renner experiment.

As in many quantum experiments which include transmission of information, there are two physicists, Alice and Bob. In this experiment, however, Alice and Bob have two friends, Amy and Brian, who are eager to find out what their respective friends have measured.

Firstly, Alice flips a coin. If it is heads, she prepares a particle with a spin value of 'down' (remember, spin results can only be 'up' or 'down'). If tails, she prepares a particle in a superposition of 'up' and 'down'. She then sends this prepared particle to Bob, in his lab. Bob measures that particle's spin value, and so now both Alice and Bob know which way up Alice's coin fell when she flipped it.

Meanwhile, Amy measures her friend Alice and her lab, and infers the result of the coin toss from this measurement. Then Brian does the same for Bob and *his* lab. After working out the mathematics, it becomes apparent that just over 8% of the time,

Amy and Brian will actually disagree about what the result of the coin toss was.

How can this be? Only one coin was ever flipped, and it must have had a single result, which was transmitted between the two labs. The difficulty arises because both Amy and Brian (both outside the labs) are making measurements on complex systems (Alice and Bob probably don't mind being described as parts of a complex system). It must be that, somewhere, the experiment has assumptions underpinning it that are not correct. There are three assumptions to look at:

1) Quantum theory is universal - everything from particles to labs follow the rules of quantum mechanics.

2) Predictions made by different agents (in this case Amy and Brian) will not contradict each other.

3) Opposite facts cannot be true. Either the coin is heads *or* it is tails.

Remember; it is not the assumptions that cause the 8% discrepancy; it is the actual mathematics of quantum mechanics - the same mathematics that has been shown to agree with observation down to as many decimal places as we can measure. It is the fact that we did not expect any disagreement between Amy and Brian that shows there is a fault in our assumptions.

Currently, no-one knows *which* of the three assumptions is wrong. Various interpretations of quantum physics strike out one or more of them.

For the Timeless Multiverse, I believe assumption number one to be correct, since if quantum physics is not universal, the scaling of events from microscopic to macroscopic becomes nonsense; quantum physics would just stop applying above a certain size and classical physics would take over. This is an interpretation called 'spontaneous collapse', which tries to save the idea of a single universe by claiming that the Copenhagen-style collapse to a single outcome occurs, only it no longer requires a measurement to cause the collapse and is governed entirely by size. Scientists have tried to prove/disprove this by making larger and larger objects remain in quantum superposition to see if they can observe this spontaneous collapse as it happens. So far, the record is two circular membranes which were about the width of a human hair in size and contained trillions of atoms. No spontaneous collapse occurred. This is because it is only the interaction with the environment that causes decoherence. Coherent objects kept in superposition can thus be as large as you like, for as long as you can maintain the superposition. It is only the difficulty of stopping the superposed objects interacting with the environment that is important.

In the Timeless Multiverse, assumption number three will be incorrect, because there will always be outcome worlds where the coin came up heads, and other worlds where it came up tails. However, for there to be a disagreement, 8% of the versions of Amy and Brian that disagree cannot remain in separate timelines. To compare their results, they must be able to share a timeline after their respective measurements have been made. This is where assumption number two becomes interesting to us. For the contradiction predicted by the experiment to occur, and be observed, in the Timeless Multiverse, both assumptions two and three must be wrong. If *only* number three was incorrect, the quantum limitations caused by entanglement that explain non-locality, would force Amy and Brian to always agree, even though it is the laws of quantum physics which show the 8% disagreement in the first place!

This is a consequence of each person experiencing their own timeline. There is yet another interpretation of quantum physics called Quantum Bayesianism (abbreviated to QBism and pronounced 'cubism') which is a 'single universe' version of each person having an individual timeline, where each person's 'observation' is considered to be a modification of that persons beliefs about possible outcomes, rather than being a real thing. So rather than two people experiencing two different timelines, they have differing beliefs inside a single universe, and these beliefs are considered to be the real things, showing that there are no lengths that people will not go to, to preserve their 'common sense' notions about the universe.

So assumption two and quantum physics cannot both be correct in the Timeless Multiverse, leaving the universality of quantum theory as the only one of the three that still applies.

When I first found out about this experiment, it was purely a thought experiment because it involves making quantum measurements on systems that themselves are doing quantum measurements, the kind of thing that normally needs quantum computers to carry out.

Now, however, a team of physicists, led by Massimiliano Proietti, have carried out the experiment using individual photons as 'observers', replacing Alice, Bob, Amy and Brian. Even with state-of-the-art apparatus, manipulating individual photons meant that they needed weeks of work to get enough results to be confident of their answers. It turns out that their results closely matched the theoretical expectations, confirming that, indeed, at least one of our basic assumptions about quantum physics must be wrong.

The question remaining is, given how complex this experiment is in quantum physics terms, could an equivalent situation arise in ordinary life? Could two people end up genuinely disagreeing on what they experienced (rather than just being mistaken)?

This is where the speculation comes in, and it's a difficult question, since many psychology experiments have shown that people's memories can be manipulated by asking questions about an event, where some or all of the questions are about things that didn't actually happen in the event. (One classic example: Someone is shown a film of an accident and asked afterwards "How fast was the white sports car going when it passed the barn while travelling along the country road?". There was no barn anywhere in the film, and yet people would still calmly make an estimate for the speed of this non-existent event!)

At the more extreme end, there is the 'Mandela Effect' where people claim to remember world and/or cultural events that didn't happen at all! It gets its name from the discovery that lots of people were convinced that the South African President Nelson Mandela had died in prison during the '80's - to the point that some of them described seeing his funeral on TV.

Let me speculate: something about the process of memory, the way we access and report that memory, is able, albeit rarely, to demonstrate the 8% contradiction inherent in the Frauchiger-Renner thought experiment. You end up in one set of worlds, but with some memories 'inherited' from a different version of yourself. The Consensus forms when different versions of people become entangled with each other and their previously separate paths have the limitations of consistency imposed on them. What this shows, on a wider scale, that it is possible for disparate world lines to come together as long as no laws of physics were violated; so if only personal information (memories) were affected. Remember: your memories are a record (if not necessarily a 100% accurate one) of the path you have navigated through the Timeless Multiverse, and this idea shows that your path is individual, despite the seeming ubiquity of the Consensus.

It also seems to me that this is the way that the retroactive magic that I described earlier, might occur. Nothing physical would contradict the observable facts, only that your set of memories contradict the current experience of the Consensus.

Near Death Experiences

Before the 1960's, if you had a cardiac arrest, you almost always died - resuscitation techniques that we take for granted now (and often see in medical dramas) did not exist. Thanks to these techniques, people now have a fighting chance to survive this previously deadly event.

When you have a cardiac arrest, your brain runs out of oxygen in about ten to fifteen seconds, and at that point, completely shuts down. The neurons in your brain reserve a tiny amount of energy in case the oxygen supply is restored, but even this runs out after five to ten minutes, and irreversible brain damage will kill you soon after that.

Why am I telling you these depressing details? Because perhaps four to five percent of the people who were successfully brought back within that crucial five to ten minute period, came back with the story of an experience they had whilst they were dead. This is known as a 'Near Death Experience' or 'NDE'.

It ought to be impossible to have any experience during a cardiac arrest. When I said the brain completely shuts down, I was not being melodramatic. The complete lack of any electrical activity in the brain is how brain death is defined, and during cardiac arrest, your brain is well and truly dead.

So what are these impossible experiences, and how do we know that (for example) the brain hasn't just invented the experience after it is brought back to life, and backdated it? (If you look at the second hand on a clock, the first second you observe passing seems to take half-a-second longer than following seconds. Your brain has backdated that first second to fill in your continuous experience)

The answer is that during that time, people have had lucid, conscious experiences that include being out of their body, where they have observed things that have happened back in 'the real world' including surgical details that they could not have possibly have known unless they were actually present. One example is the woman who needed an incision in her groin to link her up to a heart-lung machine. The nurse said "We have a problem. Her arteries are too small." The surgeon replied "Try the other side". The patient was confused because the conversation was happening at her groin when the surgery was to do with her brain. She knew nothing about the surgical procedures, but she reported it perfectly, even though she was actually brain dead at the time when the conversation took place.

This would be incredible enough, if this was the only kind of thing that these temporarily dead people experienced. Though as they say, there's more. The experience can contain some or all of a number of elements; elements that are described in similar terms in NDE's the world over. If all of these elements were included in a single NDE, it would look like this:

1) Out of body experience. May include person seeing themselves from outside, and verifiable observations as in the example above. Person feels as if all their senses, including their consciousness, are incredibly enhanced, and an overall sense that what they are experiencing is not easy or even possible to describe in normal human terms ("ineffability").

2) Person is drawn towards a point of light, which, on approaching it, becomes a tunnel of light.

3) When they emerge from the tunnel, they are in a beautiful place. (Occasionally this is a dark and frightening room instead)

4) In this place, they either observe or are met by, dead people, usually relatives (even relatives who may have died before the person was born! Accounts exist where the dead person's identity

has been subsequently verified)

5) They experience a 'life review' where they are able to not just see, but also experience any event in their life, complete with knowledge of what the other people present in the event were feeling and thinking at that time.

6) They discover a barrier or point where they realise, if they go beyond it, they will not be able to return to their body.

7) They return to their body, which is usually a horrid experience for them as they are once again in pain.

So how does this relate to magic and the Timeless Multiverse? I think there are two points to focus on. Firstly, how can a person have these kind of enhanced conscious experiences while they are literally brain dead? Secondly, the nature of the 'life review'. Here's one description of the life review from an NDE'r:

"My whole life so far appeared to be placed before me in a kind of panoramic, three-dimensional review. Throughout, I not only saw everything from my own point of view, but I also knew the thoughts of everybody who'd been involved in these events, as if their thoughts were lodged inside me. I can't say how long this life review and insight into life lasted; it may have been quite long because it covered every single subject, but at the same time it felt like a split second because I saw everything at once. It seemed as if time and distance didn't exist. I was everywhere at once, and sometimes my attention was focused on something and then I was there too."

This sounds very much as if you were able to see your 'world line' in the Timeless Multiverse from 'outside'. A similar experience is postulated in the film 'Interstellar' where the hero is taken 'out of time' and sees all possible worlds at once. Some of the NDE descriptions of their 'surroundings' throughout the experience, seem to be trying to describe what it's like to experience large numbers of dimensions with an ordinary human mind. The first step to making sense of such a picture would be to concentrate on the events you actually experienced - this would reduce the number of dimensions you need to try and build a normal 3D set of images from. Earlier, I said that being able to experience the entire Timeless Multiverse at once would be an utterly alien experience, but it might be that our normal limited viewpoint allows us to navigate such a complex structure. This attempt to make sense of massively multidimensional surroundings might also contribute to the feeling of ineffability, although I have also heard it argued that we cannot define consciousness because we have no metaphors for it; there is nothing like it that we can compare it to. This might also be true of such an unusual experience as an NDE.

Now we return to the first point: How can people be having these experiences at all? Their brains are definitely dead for a short time, and a number of the NDE's have been positively verified to have taken place during that time of brain death.

The conclusion that is most widespread (apart from "don't know" of course) is that consciousness is not actually located in the brain, and that the brain is more like a receiver for consciousness instead of a generator. As crazy as that sounds, the observations make it a pretty straightforward possible conclusion. The brain is dead, but the person is not just conscious, they feel that their consciousness has expanded and their senses are enhanced.

My speculation on this matter is probably even more mad than this idea that consciousness is a universal field that we tap into. If (as I believe) consciousness requires a brain to 'run on' - where is that brain, when the brain we associate with our consciousness is clearly not working?

The Timeless Multiverse contains countless copies of yourself, in many different branches, in both the past and the future of those branches. My thought is that the NDE you have, that experience is running on another set of brains, on a copy of yourself where you are not currently dead, but your normal waking consciousness is clearly not up and running - perhaps in a dream state. Something about the circumstances of temporary brain death can trigger this strange 'ultra dream' where they are privy to objective details about the Timeless Multiverse that would not normally be possible to access. If you had this access to countless versions of yourself (and indeed, countless versions of everyone) wouldn't this look to you like some kind of all-permeating field of consciousness?

For me, nothing throws the idea of 'running' on another version of ourselves into sharp relief, more than the reports from the small number of blind people who have had NDE's. One of these was Vicki, who had been born blind, and had her NDE because of a severe car accident. She had a brief glimpse of the accident itself, and then she was above her body in the emergency room. Because she had never seen herself, she only recognised it was her body by her wedding ring and her hair. She then went on to meet dead relatives and friends, as in other NDE's, but she could see them.

What intrigues me about this, is that when congenitally blind people have been given sight, (usually through cataract operations) they have had to spend time learning how to see, taking anywhere from a week to a few months - to tell, for example, that the cube they were seeing was the same as the cube they felt in their hand.

Vicki was scared by the fact she was suddenly seeing, but she didn't need to learn how to do it. This implies to me that her consciousness was running on a version of herself that already knew how to see.

We already know that magical experiences, including telepathy and synchronicity, happen most readily when the conscious mind is suppressed to some degree. So now, we have a situation where the entire mind is suppressed, and, in that situation, you then have roughly a 5% chance of experiencing a magical act of extraordinary proportions. All you have to do is survive the experience.

Dark Matter

If you've read anything about dark matter, (or even if you haven't) you might wonder what it has to do with magic. When I discovered the Timeless Multiverse model, I realised that rebuilding the way we look at the entire cosmos would have consequences for certain questions that scientists have about the universe. I am not a cosmologist, but I ended up reading a lot about cosmology - if only because it contains a remarkable number of things that are important to understanding the universe, things that we just don't know. Dark matter is one of these. Supposedly, there is much more of it than normal matter and it has far-reaching consequences in the creation and subsequent evolution of the universe.

So, what is this dark matter? The short answer is, no-one really knows. All we have are a series of observations which we explain by something we call 'dark matter'. So far, more success has been had discovering what it isn't, rather than what it is!

The story of dark matter started in 1933 when an astronomer, Fritz Zwicky, found that the individual galaxies in a cluster of galaxies were moving too fast to remain in a cluster. What this meant was that there needs to be more gravitational attraction (which normally means more mass, since General Relativity tells us that gravity is caused by mass warping space-time) than can be accounted for by the masses of all the visible matter in those galaxies. This strange observation went more or less unnoticed until the late 1960's when the astronomer Vera Rubin discovered that the same thing was true for individual galaxies. The rotational velocity of the stars of that galaxy ought to slow down as they get further away from the galactic centre, but in reality, their rotational velocity speeds up towards a maximum. Like this:

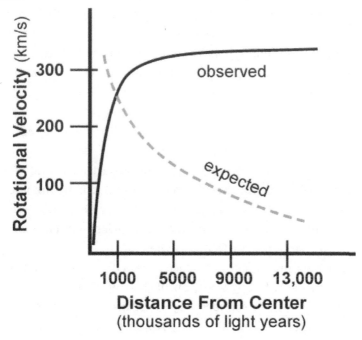

This again implies that each galaxy somehow contains more mass, generating more gravity, than all the visible mass in that galaxy. Think of each of those stars as a ball on a string. As you rotate it around your head like a lasso, the string is the gravity keeping the star in orbit. Rotating the ball too fast would cause the string to break, and the ball to fly off. This is what *should* happen to stars in galaxies, if there was no influence from dark matter to increase the strength of the 'string'. The graph above seems to imply that there is a 'halo' of dark matter surrounding the galaxy to keep the stars spinning around the galaxy as fast as they do.

So dark matter is *something* that only affects matter gravitationally. It can't be seen, but it's producing a lot of gravity.

This implies that if it is a kind of matter (although it's now more or less been ruled out that dark matter is any kind of normal matter that just doesn't emit light), there must be an awful lot of it - calculations show that dark matter makes up about 23% of the universe. Normal matter makes up about 5%. (The other 72% is *another* completely mysterious substance called 'dark energy' - about which we know even less than dark matter. All we know about dark energy, is that it's forcing the universe to expand faster than we expected - and forcing the rate of that expansion to speed up over time)

So what does this unknown 23% of dark matter mean to the Timeless Multiverse model? To tell the story, we need to reconstruct our model in a different way.

There is a theory about the construction of particles (and thus the universe) called 'string theory'. When you consider a particle to be a point, the mathematics involved in calculating what happens to particles tends to include infinities, which makes working with particles difficult. (The infinities are usually cancelled out by a mathematical process called 'renormalisation', which not everyone is happy with, but it does work.)

An alternative was proposed by Yoichiro Nambu of the University of Chicago in about 1970. Instead of point-like particles, electrons, protons and such could be considered to be loops, like tiny strings. These tiny strings would vibrate at different frequencies in a higher number of physical dimensions than we normally observe, each different combination of vibrations showing itself to us as a different particle, even though the 'strings' themselves would all be made of the same 'stuff'. (The unobservable extra dimensions are usually held to be rolled up extremely small inside our known three dimensions - think of a hosepipe; from a distance it looks like a line, but when you get close enough, you can see that another dimension is 'rolled up' in that line.)

Others put forward the idea that some of the extra dimensions could instead be very large, so that our Universe would be a four dimensional 'brane' (the term was probably derived from 'membrane', to imply a flattened, paper-thin Universe floating in three dimensions since it is not really possible to directly imagine a four dimensional Universe floating in a fifth dimension). In this picture, the dimensions that the 'brane' is embedded in are called 'the bulk'. The strings that make up the particles of our Universe would be stuck to the brane because they are almost all 'open' strings, with two ends like the strings of a guitar. There is one important exception: the graviton (which is the (as yet unobserved) carrier particle for gravity in the same way that the photon is the carrier for light) is a closed loop; it has no loose ends.

So now imagine that each section of every timeline is a brane, each with slightly different organisations of particles stuck to it, so that when you look at them in quick succession, it forms the 'flicker book' that we experience as our continuous single timeline, with our mind composed of series of brain states, one complete state stuck to each brane, part of the 'flicker book' in the same way as I explained previously. The Timeless Multiverse now looks less like a massively branching train yard, and more like a domino toppling demonstration, with all the branes lined up to follow the various pathways of the multiverse.

So far, so good. So where does dark matter come into this? As I mentioned, the graviton is not stuck to the branes, and although the mass on each brane is constantly generating gravitons, not all of them will have their effects felt on its native brane. Some will impinge on nearby branes, usually in the areas where matter already exists on that brane (since the brane it came from will have an almost identical copy of that matter).

My idea is that this 'wandering gravity' is what makes up dark matter. We know that dark matter is not any known kind of matter, and we know that the only effect it has on normal matter is gravitational. Rather than inventing a completely new kind of matter, this idea makes it easier to explain as just gravity itself - only in this case, the extra gravity is leaking in from parallel universes.

On less than galactic scales, however, the effects of this extra gravity would be so negligible as to be unmeasurable - overshadowed by the 'ordinary' gravity. Gravity is such a weak force on small scales that most scientists are sceptical that the graviton will ever be detected; a machine able to detect a single graviton would be so dense as to collapse into a black hole. The most sensitive machines in the world (for detecting gravitational waves) are required to detect the aftermath of black holes colliding; and *that* is one of the most violent gravitational events in the universe.

So is there any evidence for this extra gravity? One extremely interesting observation was made by Stacy McGaugh and his colleagues at Case Western Reserve University in Cleveland, Ohio. They remeasured the difference between the strength of gravity and the disc rotation speed of 153 spiral galaxies - the standard method of estimating how much dark matter was associated with a galaxy, as in the graph above. Where their work differed, was in the extra cross-checking they did. They compared the gravitational pull of each galaxy's visual matter with the rotation speed of nearby stars. What they found was a very close correlation between the rotation speed of the galaxies and the distribution of their visual matter. In other words, the effects of 'dark matter' depend closely on the amount and positioning of the galaxies' normal, visible matter. This was later shown to be true across a wide range of different galaxy types, which should have different dark matter distributions, and was described as 'tantamount to a natural law'. Remember; the effects of dark matter are so strong, it was expected that dark matter should dominate the ordinary stars and dust in a galaxy - not be dependent on them. By my reckoning, the parallel versions of the visible matter would be the ones generating this 'extra' gravity, which means that there needs to be several parallel universes contributing; but how many? How much more gravity would be required to reproduce the signature halo of dark matter encircling a galaxy?

Looking at the graph above, it seems that the further out from the centre of the galaxy you look, the more 'extra' gravity you need. So, if you need more gravity, there need to be more universes contributing. This implies that the further out from the centre you are, the more possible outcomes there are in that section of the Timeless Multiverse in order to produce more 'stray' gravitons. Why would this be?

The phenomenon that is responsible for more branches of the multiverse from a given point, than any other, is life. Wherever life comes into being and thrives, any living thing will result in many more outcomes than, say, a rock. The rock will do nothing except erode, over perhaps hundreds or thousands of years, whereas even an amoeba will make different choices, resulting in different sets of outcomes based on food availability and other local conditions over the course of its lifetime. And when you get to the level of intelligent life, the number of outcomes in the Timeless Multiverse that are required to encompass the behaviour of that life becomes truly enormous.

Perhaps life is more likely to evolve in the kinds of solar systems which proliferate near the edges of galaxies; something that is not entirely unlikely, because the more concentrated the matter, the more radiation and flying rocks there are likely to be. It only takes one large asteroid impact to wipe out life, or a relatively small amount of constant radiation to destroy it. Although we are only one example, our solar system is out near the edge of the galaxy, exactly where the greatest number of parallel universes are required to generate enough extra gravity to match the graph.

The upshot of this chain of speculation is that if you want to know which galaxies are most likely to contain intelligent life, look for those that have the greatest amount of dark matter.

The Function of the Orgasm

When we talked earlier about 'programming' your subconscious by finding different ways to push your conscious mind out of the way, I pointed out that the orgasm is one of the easiest ways to achieve the 'blank slate' state that this programming requires. This leads to an interesting line of speculation about the evolutionary purpose of the orgasm.

The orgasm represents, for the man, at least (and, under optimal circumstances, for the woman as well) the moment when the process of conception begins. (After the male orgasm, it takes a minimum of 45 minutes for the sperm to reach the egg)

It's possible to consider the conception of a child to be a magical act. Let's look at the best case scenario. You have the desire: the will to conceive the best possible child. You have the externalising of the desire: the sex act itself and hopefully, your partner! You have the achieving of *gnosis* at the moment of orgasm. And then afterwards, a time of relaxation and the mind wandering away.

Creating a child has a large potential for magical influence on the results. Remember; it's all about maximising the amount of entropy - both the thermodynamic entropy (any possible combination of the parents genes is available to create the child) and the informational entropy (we will have absolutely no idea which combination of genes will actually manifest). With a child, you have the creation of a single cell that can conceivably scale up to affect the whole world. Being able to maximise that potential, by magically impressing your positive expectations for your child onto the development of the egg; that would be a positive evolutionary trait.

Some ancient myths warned about the opposite - if two people did not love each other in harmony, their child would be born evil!

So when attempting to conceive a child, couples should consider it to be a magical act, a set of coincidences to be manipulated. If it doesn't spoil the mood too much, perhaps build a ritual around it so that both are in the same mindset before and after conception occurs. Of course, one difficulty is that the magical act will not be fully completed until the child is born!

Of course, some might say that it is not truly complete until the child moves out and gets a place of its own...

Conclusions

Having whisked you around a new view of the universe, used it to try and make sense of both normal magic of life and the magical magic of, well, magic, giving notes on implementing it, then finally riffing on the theme: what have I learned about the engineering of coincidence, this edge condition of normal human consciousness?

Firstly, magic is simultaneously incredibly powerful and extremely weak.

It's powerful in that you can use it to make changes to yourself and your environment that would normally be considered impossible - events which seem to be independent of time and space, events that can scale up to significant changes in your life, both physically and spiritually. Like all tools, the results you get from it depend on the use you put it to. Some use it to elevate themselves to become a better person (usually referred to in magic as 'The Great Work'), others for wealth, success, material things. These things are not good or bad in themselves; remember that magic is a tool like any other, and "It's a poor gun that doesn't point both ways". The important thing to remember is that you are carving a path for yourself, both by your normal actions and your magical actions, and the root of your magical actions is whatever belief system and expectations you have designed for yourself. As Kurt Vonnegut put it: "You are what you pretend to be. So be careful what you pretend to be."

For non-magicians, their beliefs and expectations act randomly on their environment unless they focus. People talk about being 'in the zone', where whatever they are working on becomes all-encompassing, and both the world and the normal experience of time passing, drop away. Magical practise is a method for putting your life 'in the zone'. Zen masters refer to 'enlightenment' which is to 'know thyself' to the point where you no longer need to ask questions about it; to instinctively express your true nature. Or, in terms we talked about earlier, programming your 'autopilot' with your True Will (as Aleister Crowley called it).

Magic is weak, because it is fragile and unreliable. A metaphor I usually employ is that of trying to steer a truck travelling at 60 miles per hour with no brakes.

As we saw with parapsychology, the more you use it, the smaller the overall effect. You might get a few great successes early on ("beginner's luck") or lots of small, regular successes over time (luck in general). Hence the old advice to only use magic for things that are important. If we take things like Basil Shackleton's precognition as a rule of thumb for success, you can think of it as perhaps increasing your chances by a maximum of 50%. Of course, if the thing you are attempting is almost impossible in the first place, adding 50% to that chance won't make a lot of difference. People often joke that I should have won the lottery by now. The chances of winning the lottery are (at a conservative estimate) 14 million to one. Making that chance 50% more likely increases the chance to 7,000,000 to one. In comparison, bookmakers have allowed bets on the Biblical Apocalypse occurring in any given year - at odds of 6,000 to one. By those numbers, you are still over a thousand times more likely to experience the Apocalypse than to win the lottery! More seriously, it's been estimated that your average chance of dying in a car crash are about 300 to one - so, magic or not, if you really think you are in with a chance in the lottery, you should never ride in a car again - your lottery win is over 46,000 times less likely than a fatal crash.

I often liken trying to do magic to win the lottery (or other really unlikely things) to attempting to land a jumbo jet on a ten pence piece. Why not use the magic for a more realistic sum of money from a non-specific source where your chances will be less ludicrously low? Of course you still run the risk of The Monkey's Paw: that of your wish being fulfilled in the worst possible way.

You might say, what if the magic is purely correlation and not causation? There will be a set of outcomes with the successful result in it, and a set of outcomes containing yourself, whether you did the magic to achieve that result or not. What if you ended up in the successful result area with no reference to whether you performed any magic? This would mean that the successful versions of you that performed the magic only *thought* that the magic was responsible. The problem is, of course, just as with all interpretations of quantum mechanics (as the Timeless Multiverse more or less is) it's very difficult to build experiments that are able to directly prove or disprove which particular interpretation is correct. The personal timeline nature of the Timeless Multiverse adds yet another level of difficulty to experiment - how can you get a result that everyone can agree on, if the normal process of getting everyone to agree on it (i.e. The Consensus) is also the process that is most likely to destroy any useful results? We saw when looking at the Frauchiger-Renner thought experiment how complex and delicate (even by the standards of quantum mechanics) the kind of experimental results that include magic truly are. When I started out with this project, one of the things I said was that I expected that the best we could do about magic (psi, etc.) was to prove why we couldn't prove it. Although I haven't really proved anything, I hope that I've managed to advance some way down that particular road of *why* the results are unprovable; each person's individual path may not correspond with the Consensus, especially if the individual results are 'magical'.

So what is the purpose of magic? Does it even have a use, or is it just some accidental novelty like double-jointedness or a strange obsolete thing like the remnants of a tail?

Human beings are possibility engines. We've evolved to occupy as many niches as possible; to be flexible enough to colonise whole branches of the multiverse that only a self-aware, intelligent lifeform could. To paraphrase the mathematician Kurt Gödel: "Human beings are built to be complete, rather than consistent." If we were consistent, never contradicting ourselves, we would be extremely limited indeed, more like computer programs rather than people. As the old joke goes: "If the human brain was simple enough to understand, we'd be so simple we couldn't".

The world we live in depends on continuity, yet, at the same time, the biggest changes in our world come from unexpected events. Leaving aside the peculiar blindness towards the consequences of our own actions which underlies many people's attitudes towards ecology, climate change and so on, many of the unexpected changes are unexpected because they have scaled up from initial conditions too small to see. Scaling events like these do not have 'trends' that can be analysed, regardless of whatever narrative analysts might cook up about them in hindsight. Magic gives us access to this mechanism, either to influence or predict, allowing us to colonise more branches of the multiverse than our long list of ancestors on the tree of life. Life's purpose (if you can put it that way) is to survive; you can view evolution's 'survival of the fittest' in terms of 'how many branches does this species occupy?'

So the more branches of the Timeless Multiverse we occupy, the longer and more successfully we survive as a species. Even if one set of branches comes to an unfortunate end (through disease, nuclear war etc.), there will always be others where the choices had been different, and intelligent life marches on.

Perhaps your use of magic will allow you to be on one of those branches - if it's not too late.